END ||||||||||||||||||| 'S

In *The Prophetic Voice of God*, Lana Vawser generously offers the fruit of her journey of intimacy with the Father. What a gift! It has been decades in the making. As a result, we are able to benefit from her hunger and single-minded pursuit of His presence. Each story and insight draws us into a deeper relationship with God, so that we know—with certainty—His heart for the world. Read this book, and let the encounters draw you into a greater experience of God's delight over you, that you might know His goodness first-hand. From there, you will be able to explore the creative ways He pursues His children.

BILL JOHNSON
Bethel Church, Redding, CA
Author of *God is Good* and *When Heaven Invades Earth*

What a refreshing read! Lana's book *The Prophetic Voice of God* takes a very personal and balanced look at the way God speaks to us and is an encouragement to us all to lean in to the affectionate love of God. I love the way Lana emphasizes the value and importance of intimacy with the Lord as our highest call. We are all invited into a deeply personal relationship with God, to be rooted and grounded in His love, and from the place of being secure in His heart He wants to love others through us in practical and supernatural ways. Developing the prophetic anointing to be a blessing to others is an overflow of our connection to God and His deep love for us. I believe this book will inspire and encourage you to walk and talk with the Lord so that you too can hear and enjoy His loving voice.

KATHERINE RUONALA
Author, *Living in the Miraculous*, *Wilderness to Wonders*,
and *Life with the Holy Spirit*
Senior leader of Glory City Church Brisbane
GCN International founder and facilitator of the Australian
Prophetic Council

I truly believe that Lana Vawser's life is a sign and a wonder for the body of Christ for today. What I loved about *The Prophetic Voice of God* is that she explains how God not only speaks to us through His written Word but also through dreams, visions, and unusual signs that can occur in our everyday lives. She writes about her persistence and hunger to seek God in a secret place, which results in amazing encounters. She is a great example for those who are called into a prophetic ministry. This is a timely book to inspire a new breed of prophets to *soar as eagles*. I salute you, Lana. You are inspiration for many.

ADAM F THOMPSON
Prophetic ministry and international author
www.voiceoffireministries.org

The first time I met Lana, I knew that she was a woman of godly virtue, integrity, and prophetic accuracy. I honor and respect her deeply. Her book, *The Prophetic Voice of God,* is solid, foundational, and inspirational. It is a handbook that is both profound and practically written for those who are hungry to engage in hearing and proclaiming the prophetic words of God. It was written for you.

DR. PATRICIA KING
Founder, Patricia King Ministries
www.patriciaking.com

Lana's heart for hearing the voice of God has inspired people all over the world to not only listen to His voice but also discover it for themselves. This book, *The Prophetic Voice of God*, will become one of the keys of the Kingdom that Jesus will use to unlock His voice to generations of people.

MATT BECKENHAM
Senior Pastor
Haberfield Baptist Church
www.haberfieldbaptist.org.au

I regard it my privilege to endorse *The Prophetic Voice of God* by Lana Vawser. I have known Lana for quite a number of years and have watched the way our Lord has taken her gift and used that gift to encourage countless people right around our world. Lana, I believe, is a gifted prophet who hears the voice of God. I believe what she has written in this book will be of great encouragement to those who take the time to read it. I am so glad she has followed the Lord's leading in her life.

GREG BECKENHAM
Dare To Believe Ministries

As one of Lana's closest friends for almost 15 years, I can honestly say that these words reveal her true heart and overflowing passion of her life's greatest pursuit, Jesus. Through the testimony of her personal journey, Lana lays herself bare—raw, vulnerable, and transparent—to inspire others to hunger after not only the prophetic voice of God, but His divine presence, intimacy, and deep love. These keys, revelations, and impartations of her powerful gift, coupled with the practical applications, can see His prophetic voice flourish in your life too!

NATALIE FULLER
www.tenaciousmama.com

Lana's unique style of transparent expression through testimony and teaching on hearing God's voice will meet and inspire every believer in any stage of their Christian walk. Her refreshing, out-of-the-box approach to relationship and intimacy with the Lord sends the invitation to every child of God into the endless creativity of the ways that He speaks, while simultaneously invoking a hunger and thirst to go deeper in pursuit of His heart. Be refreshed, be inspired, and be provoked as you encounter His heart in new ways within the pages of this book.

ANITA ALEXANDER
Revival Flame Ministries
www.revival-flame.org

Lana Vawser carries a heart-piercing voice of purity that speaks heaven's whispers and invites, even compels, intimate conversations with the Father. Her heart is to translate the creative language of heaven within these pages. Lana imparts wisdom into your prophetic journey, but more profoundly this book infuses childlike joy, creative vision, and stirs contagious hunger to enjoy the divine, and never boring, conversation with God.

JODIE HUGHES
Pour It Out Ministries
pouritout.org
www.facebook.com/jodiehuges.pouritout

I've fondly referred to Lana Vawser as a prophetic "bubbling brook," meaning she's a trusted prophet of the Lord who bubbles forth His word like a flowing and refreshing river. I'm so excited to read and reread her book, *The Prophetic Voice of God*, knowing that the ease of her flow today is the result of a deep personal journey and long-term learning by the Spirit of God. As you read her process into accurately hearing and releasing the prophetic voice of God, you will be taught, challenged, and encouraged. Not only that, but your heart will be awakened to a whole new world, this book providing you a road map to journey deep into the prophetic voice of God.

JENNIFER EIVAZ
Founder, Harvest Ministries International
Executive Pastor, Harvest Christian Center, Turlock, CA
Author, *Seeing the Supernatural* and *The Intercessors' Handbook*

Lana Vawser is one of the most prolific writers and accurate prophetic voices of our day. *The Prophetic Voice of God* is by far one of the most powerful and inspiring books I have ever read. Written as a labor of love, it is a golden treasury of wisdom that will transform your life. Lana's extraordinary journey of romancing God will draw you deeper into the Father's heart and create a greater measure of His abiding presence and beauty within you.

GARY BEATON
TransformationGloryMinistries.org
Founder, Transformation Glory Ministries
Writer, speaker, prophetic voice to the nations

During the darkest season of my life, I met Lana Vawser. Although we had never met in person, the Holy Spirit spoke through her into the deepest places of my heart. The power of His word through her voice left me astonished and wondering how she could hear so clearly! This book answers that question!

In *The Prophetic Voice of God*, Lana shares with each of us the key that unlocks the door to the wonder of His world. It contains fresh revelation that will draw you into a new place of intimacy with Jesus and teaches you how to live your life led by the Voice.

KAREN WHEATON
The Ramp
Hamilton, AL

I have known Lana Vawser to be a sincere and passionate prophetic voice to the nations. In this book she perfectly unpacks revelation and practical application about hearing the voice of God. As with all solid prophetic writings, Lana emphasizes relationship with Jesus as a cornerstone of prophetic ministry. She charges the reader to go deeper in their personal walk with God and brilliantly equips them to effectively walk out a prophetic lifestyle! This is a must read for every prophetic person and those who want to hear more clearly.

RYAN LESTRANGE
ryanlestrange.com
RLM, TRIBE Network, and
best-selling author of *Supernatural Access*

If you need encouragement and to receive a fresh word from the Lord then Lana Vawser's book, *The Prophetic Voice of God*, is for you. It will activate you to hear the voice of God in your daily life. It is full of personal experiences, teaching, and prophetic insight into how God is speaking in the new millennium. This is a new wineskin for hearing God birthed out of passion for His presence.

DOUG ADDISON
DougAddison.com

The best books—the VERY BEST BOOKS—on The Voice of God, must, by necessity, be loaded with personal stories, amazing encounters with God, and almost-unbelievable tales of miraculous divine appointments. Lana Vawser's book has all of these and much more. Expect to hear stories about great success, but let me encourage you that with this book, Lana also is completely transparent with stories of her own failures and insecurities too. And from my chair, that catapults this book close to the #1 status of books about learning to hear God's voice. Get this book, and buy one for a friend while you're at it!

STEVE SHULTZ
Founder and President of The Elijah List

PUBLISHER'S NOTE

THIS IS THE KIND OF BOOK THAT DESTINY IMAGE EXISTS TO publish. Let me rephrase: Lana Vawser is the kind of author that, I believe, Don Nori Sr. saw in his spirit as he was pioneering Destiny Image as publisher for the prophets back in 1982.

Lana is a powerful example of a company of "times and seasons" prophets the Lord is raising up in this hour. And what I admire most about Lana, as a friend, is that she is a relational, everyday person. She's a wife and a mother. She's a writer, blogger, and faithful communicator of the now word of the Lord. She communicates prophetic words with authenticity, integrity and authority.

What a joy it is for us to present this book to you. More than information, I believe there is an impartation on these pages that will open your spiritual eyes and ears to the unique ways the Holy Spirit communicates. Many believers are straining to hear His voice in this hour, but what Lana's book makes very clear is this: the Holy Spirit is creative and unique in His methods of communication. It's time to stop our religious straining and rather, start resting in the multi-dimension ways that God has hardwired us to hear from Heaven.

Get ready to embark on a joyful prophetic adventure!

LARRY SPARKS, MDIV.
Publisher, Destiny Image

THE PROPHETIC

VOICE
OF GOD

**LEARNING TO RECOGNIZE
THE LANGUAGE OF THE HOLY SPIRIT**

LANA VAWSER

DESTINY IMAGE® PUBLISHERS, INC.

P.O. Box 310, Shippensburg, PA 17257-0310

"Promoting Inspired Lives."

This book and all other Destiny Image and Destiny Image Fiction books are available at Christian bookstores and distributors worldwide.

Cover design by Eileen Rockwell

Interior design by Terry Clifton

For more information on foreign distributors, call 717-532-3040.

Reach us on the Internet: www.destinyimage.com.

ISBN 13 TP: 978-0-7684-1803-3

ISBN 13 eBook: 978-0-7684-1804-0

ISBN 13 HC: 978-0-7684-1806-4

ISBN 13 LP: 978-0-7684-1805-7

For Worldwide Distribution, Printed in the U.S.A.

7 8 / 22

DEDICATION

Jesus, it's all because of You and it's all for You! Forever I will live my life in thankfulness for all you have done. This is for you, may your name be glorified and lifted high! Thank you for the precious gift we are given in the invitation to know You and hear Your voice. Coffees with You are my favorite place! Because of You, I am never the same and forever changed! It's all the work of Your hand!"

"Your ability to hear from God does not replace the prophet, nor does the prophet replace your ability to hear from God."
—BILL JOHNSON

CONTENTS

FOREWORD

GET READY TO BEGIN YOUR PERSONAL JOURNEY OF HEARING the Father's voice! You are about to embark on an amazing, life-filled journey. It's your time to come away with Him. He is drawing you. All that you have experienced up to now has been to deepen your hunger for Him. Deep is calling out to deep. The depth of His heart is calling out to the depths of your inner being. Lies and limitations are being broken off as you enter in to the joy of knowing Him more intimately. The season of your life has changed. A spiritual "springtime" has come. It is your season to draw near to God and to hear His whisper.

God longs that all His children hear His voice. Jesus told us that His sheep will hear His voice. And the voice of the Holy Spirit must be heard as He speaks clearly to His churches. The Trinity speaks. God will not be silent. He will speak and you will hear Him! You will be lead into a place of hungering and thirsting for more of the one your soul loves. Your heart will be awakened to receive the wonder of His love and His marvelous ways as He works it out through your life. You'll also be encouraged as you hear some of Lana Vawser's amazing encounters and some simple things she did to develop a life of encountering Him over and over. She will uncover some of the mysteries of His ways for you so that you too will begin to recognize Him when He comes to you.

There are many today who are just waiting to be told that's it's alright to move in the supernatural realm. Beloved, don't wait a day longer. Begin your journey to listen, as a lover would listen to the Beloved. He longs to meet with you and share His heart with you on a daily basis. In this book, God will lead you into understanding *The Prophetic Voice of God*.

Lana has made it simple to follow by being vulnerable, personal, and engaging. She shares her own journey and inspires you with her own testimony. You will begin to view every day as a new, fresh day of walking and talking with your Lord as she teaches you how to activate your heart to the point that you begin looking and listening for Him to come wherever you are. And even though none of us start out overnight understanding, as Lana puts it, "it's a process." You'll learn how to become like a child again and how to posture your heart and position yourself to hear, for He has secrets saved up for you that He's longed to tell you.

She will show you scripture after scripture and example after example from God's heroes of the faith, using their encounters to show you through the legitimacy of the scriptures. Yes, you have God's permission. He's longing for you to hear His voice. And you won't doubt it again as she walks you through the Word. For the Father desires to give you the Kingdom and to give you more than you have dreamed and have imagined! He's just been waiting for you to desire what He's waiting for you to receive. He wants to make your dreams come alive.

Lana lays her heart out before you in the pages of this masterful book, walking you through difficulty, giving you a road map out. And after each time you will find your heart soaring above all the fear and doubt that the enemy tries to put in your heart and mind. You'll learn the difference between the voice of the enemy and the voice of the Father. And you'll begin to move into a place of discernment so that you understand whose voice you're hearing.

With the skill of an anointed prophet, she will walk you through some of her own dark days and how God broke in and spoke to her. And she'll share her own days of wondering if she had missed Him, doubting the very words that He had spoken to her and how she overcame. Your spirit will begin to come alive and your ears will begin to open. As Lana says, "God's words bring us to the place where our reality is supernatural." The Father's heart for you is to experience the totality of life and His fullness with nothing holding you back from Him and from hearing His voice!

Who could ever explain the wonder of [God's] decisions or search out the mysterious way he carries out His plans? (Romans 11:33)

We can! We can search it out and we can carry out His plans according to His Word and according to His words! Thanks to the Father and thanks to Holy Spirit who lives within us!

So get ready! You're about to embark on an exciting journey into the very heart of the Father. It will change your outlook on life and yourself. It will transform you in ways that you never expected. He's about to reveal His glory and His heart of love to the world through *you* in new and amazing ways. He is calling you to enter the secret place of His heart where you will develop ears that hear, eyes that see, and a heart that discerns His love. For He is longing to share His mysterious ways with you. He's ready for you to enter into your Kingdom birthright by learning to recognize His voice. He is longing for a deeper relationship with you, but until your spiritual ears, your spiritual eyes, and your heart are open you will never be able to fully enter in. Have fun reading this awesome book and receiving the impartation that it carries! I predict that you will not only love it, but will need to purchase a copy for others as well! Enjoy reading *The Prophetic Voice of God!*

BRIAN and CANDICE SIMMONS
The Passion Translation Project
www.passionmovement.com

CHAPTER 1

THE BIRTHPLACE OF THE PROPHETIC VOICE

As I sought the Lord's heart for this book, I felt His heart of joy and adventure. The adventure every day of seeking His heart and hearing His voice. The joy it is daily to connect with His heart, to hear His whispers of love and truth, and to grow in our understanding of the language of the Spirit. God speaks differently to each of us, and each moment He speaks is an *invitation into encounter.*

Every time He speaks, we are invited into a deeper place of intimacy to engage with His heart and what He is dreaming about and speaking. It's the most beautiful place. It's the place where our hearts are awakened by His kisses of truth, by His winds of wisdom, by His refreshing revelation. The words that flow from

His mouth and resound from His heart *are* life (see Matt. 4:4). Jesus Christ is our life, and His Word and what He speaks is our true *reality*.

For many, there has been so much fear and trepidation around hearing the voice of God because, "What if what I am hearing is not God?" "What if I miss it?" "What if I step in the wrong direction on something that I heard and it turned out not to be God?" So many of these questions are birthed out of fear and anxiety. I feel that through this book, the Lord wants to *break* the fear of hearing from Him off you. He wants to awaken you to greater joy and the childlike wonder that comes from hearing His voice and grow in understanding how He is speaking.

Whether you are just beginning your journey to seek out how to hear from God or you know and understand how the Lord speaks, I prophesy over you today that there are new depths of His heart to be explored as you understand the prophetic voice of God. God is always speaking, and my prayer is that as you read through the pages of this book you will live even more intentionally and actively awakened to being tuned in, leaning in, positioned and looking for Him everywhere.

God is very unique in the way He speaks and how differently He speaks. As you read these pages, my prayer is that any boxes, limitations, or lies that you have believed about the way God speaks and what He might say to you if you lean in really close— all ceilings and limitations that would hinder your journey of hearing from God—will be suddenly broken off you. Excitement will ignite within you for the new depths of His heart that are before you, ready to be explored.

"My Sheep Hear My Voice"

First and foremost, I want you to know that God still speaks. He wants to speak to you, you can hear Him, and you are about to embark on a journey of hearing from Him in ways you have never imagined. He still speaks today, and He has much He wants to say to you.

> *My own sheep will hear my voice and I know each one, and they will follow me* (John 10:27).

You are a sheep! His precious sheep! So that's your promise right there, that you can and will hear His voice.

> *Ask me and I will tell you remarkable secrets you do not know about things to come* (Jeremiah 33:3 NLT).

That's an invitation! An invitation into hearing remarkable secrets about things you don't know. So it's an ever-increasing journey.

The word *remarkable* strikes me! It means "worthy of attention, striking." Synonyms include extraordinary, exceptional, amazing, astonishing, astounding, marvelous, wonderful, sensational, stunning, incredible, unbelievable, miraculous, phenomenal, striking, outstanding, momentous, impressive, memorable, unforgettable, noteworthy, great, important, rare, surprising, fantastic, terrific, tremendous, stupendous, awesome, out of this world, wondrous.

That sounds like an amazing, *fun,* and *life-filled* journey to me—and that was and has been my experience! Come for a walk with me through these next pages and let me tell you where it began for me.

Over the years of seeking His heart and growing in hearing from Him, in my journey through the breakthroughs and the breakdowns, I have learned so much. One thing I have learned and continue to learn every day is that one word from Him changes everything! There is an incredible battle that takes place over our journey to hear from God because the enemy wants to hinder you and keep you from the place of deep intimacy with Jesus.

YOUR GREATEST WEAPON

I love what I heard Graham Cooke say at a conference: *"Your intimacy with Jesus is your greatest weapon."* That's where it all began for me.

Growing up I had such a longing and drawing to Jesus. As a young girl I would sit in front of the television at Easter and Christmas, and I would watch movie after movie about Jesus. Such a love for Him filled my heart. In 1996, I met Him—beautiful Jesus! My life was radically transformed by the peace that I felt the moment I met Him. I remember so clearly the unexplainable peace, joy, hope, and excitement that filled my heart.

From the moment I got saved, I had an incredible passion and hunger to hear from Him. I had such love for Jesus, such a deep yearning and longing to know Him, and my heart burned within me to hear from Him.

> *They asked each other, "Were not our hearts burning within us while he talked with us on the road and opened the Scriptures to us?"* (Luke 24:32 NIV)

The passion to hear His voice burned in me day and night. That's when I began to position myself to hear from Him. I became very well acquainted with my bedroom floor! I had been told that the *only way* the Lord speaks is through His Word. Absolutely, He speaks through His Word, but there was a deep yearning in my heart to be engaged so deeply with Him that every minute of every day, no matter where I was, I would hear Him speak and see Him moving. Besides Jesus, my favorite biblical character was always Joseph. I was drawn to the story of Joseph and how God spoke to him in his dreams (see Gen. 37). Later on in his life, he was positioned in different places to engage with the heart of God and interpret what the Lord was saying through dreams.

The fire in me continued to burn. The cry of my heart was, "There has to be more!" Day and night He would show up, and His presence was so strong, His power so tangible, that I would weep for hours in His presence as He filled me with His Spirit. He was so close, like waves crashing over me, one after another. His love was so thick, so warm, so life-giving and soothing like honey. I would encounter His heart night after night, yet I would hear nothing.

Day after day, the hunger to hear from Him rose so much that I began to get discouraged. I would spend so long in the Word, but that "light bulb moment" just hadn't happened. I never felt my breath taken away from knowing deep in the core of me that the King of kings and Lord of lords just spoke to me.

Until one night.

He showed up again! His presence was so heavy, His power flowing through my body so strongly. I never wanted to leave. And then I heard a whisper, so quiet in my ears, yet so loud in my heart: *"I love you!"*

Those three little words catapulted me into a journey of discovery. A journey of deep intimacy like I had never experienced before. Every day, I would wake and feel the invitation to *"come away"* and be with Him and hear what was on His heart. It really was the invitation into the divine dance of His heart. To be drawn in so close, to hear the rhythm of His heartbeat and partner with it. To be in the place of intimacy with Him where the words from His heart and the whispers of His love brought me to life over and over again. Each word flowing from His mouth was like the shock from a defibrillator bringing the dry, dead places of my heart to life. Each word was like honey, soothing the hurting places, the places where the enemy had whispered his lies to cage me and keep me from my beloved. Everything suddenly started to rattle and shake as I would hear such words of love and truth fill my heart. The chains began to fall off one by one as His words of truth enveloped my heart and soul and His Word came down like a hammer.

> *"Does not my word burn like fire?" says the Lord.*
> *"Is it not like a mighty hammer that smashes a rock*
> *to pieces?"* (Jeremiah 23:29 NLT)

This season changed my life. The season of great awakening. The realization that He longed to speak to me and I could live *daily* in that place of deep communion with Him. He actually invites me into a place of such deep communion that I get to hear His secrets—what He is dreaming about for me, my life, and the lives of others.

> *There's a private place reserved for the lovers of God,*
> *where they sit near Him and receive the revelation-*
> *secrets of His promises* (Psalm 25:14).

YOUR POSITIONING IS KEY

No matter what my day entailed, every afternoon I would feel His invitation to "walk with Him." I began to awaken to the truth of this glorious journey before me of intimacy with Jesus and hearing His voice. In that season and every season thereafter, the *key* for me was *my positioning.*

I let go of the striving and "trying to hear" and the anxiety that brought, and I simply abandoned myself to be with Him. Whether I heard anything or not. I was chasing after His heart and His presence, spending time with Him, loving on Him, ministering to Him with my worship whether I heard anything or not. The invitation into the divine romance took my hunger to an even greater level—hunger for the closeness of His presence and His power that flowed through me and touched me. It was a fire that burned in me so strongly that I cried out to Him, "Even if You don't speak to me, I will chase after You!" I was moving to the place of just enjoying Him. Like having a cup of coffee with a friend and enjoying their presence and learning about them, so it was with Him. A whole new journey opened up before me. My hunger for Jesus catapulted me into some of the greatest adventures of my life with Him.

COFFEE WITH JESUS

So there I was, my heart burning with the words that I had heard from His heart. That whisper was so clear in my heart and rung in my ears—so soft, so loving, so tender, yet so loud and weighty that like thunder it would cause mountains to tremble. The peace that came from hearing those three little words, *"I love you,"* was like nothing I had ever experienced.

> *God thunders with His voice wondrously, doing great things which we cannot comprehend* (Job 37:5 NASB).

11

So with my heart burning, I chased Him. Every afternoon I would walk through the luscious green fields, the wide-open spaces, near where I lived—the wind blowing against my face and through my hair as I cried out to Him to know Him. I was so hungry for Him, I decided to *make even more room in my life for Him to speak and meet with me,* so I began my weekly coffee dates with Jesus. I took my Bible and my journal and I sat in a café for hours on end, imagining Jesus sitting on the other side of the table, and I asked questions. These questions became the tipping point of my walk with Him.

"What are You dreaming about today, Jesus?"

"What do You want to say to me today?"

In the quiet little café with the aroma of freshly brewed coffee rising out of my mug, I found the place of being completely undone—undone by love.

As I asked Him the two questions burning in my heart, a sense overwhelmed me so strongly. It was as if this strong feeling was shouting, *"Pick up your pen and write."*

I picked up my pen and opened my journal to a fresh, crisp, clean page. This heralded the beginning of a completely new chapter of my life—a new chapter of intimacy. I took a deep breath and felt like a tidal wave just began to flow through my hand.

I began to write line after line after line of beautiful truth. I wrote so quickly that at times my hand could not keep up. The pages were wet with my tears as I wrote, knowing the moment had come. I was in a holy space, a divine moment of connecting with His heart, and truth poured out.

"How delighted I am in you."

"I am so proud of you."

"You are My beautiful daughter; I rejoice over you with singing."

I was suddenly immersed in and surrounded by love and acceptance like I had never known on this earth. The tears poured down from my face; my hands were charged with power; my writing was so scribbly because I could not keep up with the waterfall of declarations of truth pouring out over me. My heart exploded with joy as I wrote. *"It's Him! He's speaking!"* I knew with every fiber of my being that I had connected with the heart of God. I wrote page after page after page of promises until my hand came to rest and I knew He was done.

I looked down at my journal, and through tears I saw a beautiful love letter from heaven to me. A letter like one written to a little girl from a proud father. This letter of love, my very own, was from my Father in heaven *to me*.

Fear was a giant in my life that suffocated me in so many ways, especially when hearing from God. So the moment of doubt crept in: *"Was that just me? Did I make that up?"* Within a moment I came to my senses. Every line spoken I could have added a Bible verse to. It was such beautiful truth, and with every word *I came alive!* Such love and such peace like I had never experienced. Every word ignited a fire in my heart and soul that could not be contained. Coffees with Jesus became my favorite parts of the week.

The invitation from His heart continued to beckon me: *"Come away and be with Me."* I longed to be with Him. Afternoons became a great delight as I walked with Him through luscious green fields, up and down hills, and I would ask Him questions. For years and years of coffee dates and afternoon walks, He showed me His relentless pursuit of me and my heart. He unveiled to me His yearning heart that longed to speak to me more than I wanted to hear. I realized that my hunger for Him attracted Him.

I realized that He wasn't waiting for me to "get it right" and then He would speak. I was awakened to the revelation that He is a God who is so longing for deeper relationship with me that He would work in me, calibrate my heart, teach me sensitivity, and *journey with me* to hear from Him.

On this journey, all of the swirling questions, *"Does He still speak today? Does He only speak through the Word?"* were so clearly answered. He absolutely speaks through His Word, but I now understood that He also speaks in the still, small voice.

> *After the earthquake came a fire, but the Lord was not in the fire. And after the fire came a gentle whisper* (1 Kings 19:12 NIV).

Day after day, week after week, He would whisper words of truth to me. He began to speak to me about my destiny and what I was called to, igniting in me the desire to partner with Him to see the world changed for Jesus. As His whispers became more and more frequent, like injections of hope and life, I realized something significant about what happens when He speaks. When He speaks, it activates my *faith* and my ability to *dream*. Every time He speaks, His whispers bring me to life, catapult me into greater freedom, and ignite in me the spark of Matthew 19:26:

> *Jesus looked at them and said, "With man this is impossible, but with God all things are possible"* (NIV).

The calibration happened little by little through each whisper I heard, each verse I read, each story about Jesus and His life, each way He spoke to me on that journey. He was calibrating my perspective, my reality. Every word that flowed from His mouth and heart *always brought me up higher*. Every word cheered me on in this journey taking me from glory to glory, and His plans for me were so much greater than I realized (see 2 Cor. 3:18; Jer. 29:11). It was beyond anything I had ever hoped, imagined, or dreamed.

> *That is what the Scriptures mean when they say, "No eye has seen, no ear has heard, and no mind has imagined what God has prepared for those who love him"* (1 Corinthians 2:9 NLT).

> *Never doubt God's mighty power to work in you and accomplish all this. He will achieve infinitely more than your greatest request, your most unbelievable dream, and exceed your wildest imagination! He will outdo them all, for his miraculous power constantly energizes you* (Ephesians 3:20).

HE SPEAKS, THINGS SHIFT

His words *shift* our reality and bring us into *His* reality. The truth is that He speaks; the words from His heart are always leading you and me into the truth that our reality is and should daily be:

> *He answered, "The Scriptures say: Bread alone will not satisfy, but true life is found in every word, which constantly goes forth from God's mouth"* (Matthew 4:4).

God's words bring us to the place where our reality is the supernatural—it's what Jesus says to us, about us, through us, and for us. Learning how to hear His voice and discerning and understanding how He speaks is one of the most powerful weapons He has given us. As we hear, live in, and live from the words that He speaks, the circumstances around lose their power to shake us. We can be people who live in a place of hope despite storms; we can be the eagles He has called us to be, who live "high above" what we walk through on this earth. We can be people who know how to live in peace—the peace that surpasses all understanding—despite the wind, waves, and storms that roar. From the place of divine romance with Him, we live as overcomers, feasting daily upon His *rhema* and *logos* words to us.

When He speaks, His truth confronts. It exposes lies. It exposes limitations; it exposes containments. Like a proud Father on the sidelines watching His children running a race, His voice is the *constant*. It's the constant place of life, encouragement, and hope. When we trip, stumble, or fall, His voice surrounds us, calls us up and out of our current circumstance, and shifts our perspective.

The journey to hear the voice of God and understand how He speaks is the most powerful place. Your garden place, your secret place with Him, your "dates" with Jesus—these are where you come alive to His goodness, His kindness, and His love. You become fully present and awake to who you are and all He has called you to. It's in His presence! It's your communion with Him! It's your confidence that He speaks to you and you can recognize His voice.

None of us have arrived. None of us can claim we are "experts" in hearing from God, and let us never come to that place. We are all still learning, we are all still searching, we are all still yielding—leaning in and allowing Him to recalibrate our ears to hear, our hearts to discern, our eyes to see.

If you're feeling the pressure, the anxiety, the fear that can creep in when we really seek to hear from God—if you've had disappointments in the past or times when you thought you heard God and you missed it—I release healing over you right now in the name of Jesus. I pray that the Holy Spirit would minister to that part of your heart and soul, and that even as you read these words right now His sweet, beautiful presence would heal you and speak His truth to you. That you would have the courage to stand again, to lean in, to trust again, and to seek Him again. That you would free-fall again into His arms as you continue to read the pages of this book; and your eyes would open wider than ever before, your ears would hear Him in ways you never have, and hope would be restored to you.

Wherever you are on your journey of hearing from God, it's great to be on this journey of learning with you. Seeking His heart and His voice invites us deeper into knowing Him; it reveals His nature, the language of the Spirit, and the way He speaks—His creativity (which I absolutely adore and we will discuss in Chapter 3).

I decree a new level of adventure and intimacy with Him over your life. I decree joy over you as you continue to seek Him and hear His heart for you, your family, your circumstances, and the world. Every word you hear from Him will undo you all over again with His love and kindness and the "bigger than you can ever imagine" plans He has for you and the remarkable secrets He has to share with you.

As we continue to move through these chapters together, my prayer for you echoes Revelation 3:18: *"Purchase eye salve to be placed over your eyes so that you can truly see."* Invite the Holy Spirit to teach you to hear so that you may live in the reality of Matthew 13:16: *"But blessed are your eyes because they see, and your ears because they hear"* (NIV).

I have shared the beginning of my journey. (Don't worry, there is a lot more to come!) His story for you is bigger than you, and it all starts at the place of the divine romance—the dance of intimacy, the Song of Songs place of encounter and walking in the garden with Him, the coffees with Jesus. His truth setting you free is not just for you, but it's for the world. Like one of my inspirations, Bill Johnson, says, "We owe the world an encounter with God."

The secret place is your birthing place!

A whole new depth of adventure in hearing from Him is before you. I'm excited for you and what He is going to show you.

Grab a coffee, and I'll see you in Chapter Two!

PRAYER

Lord, I love You and I want to know You more. Take me deeper than I have ever been. Lead me deeper into Your heart and the secret place, that I may know You more intimately than ever before. Teach me in greater ways how to be still before You, to position myself before You, to see You, to know You, and to encounter Your heart. In Jesus's name, amen.

ACTIVATION

Take some time to sit alone with the Lord today and enjoy Him. Cultivate your secret place today.

DECREE

I am created for intimacy with God; He loves to spend time with me and know me. He loves to reveal His heart and Word to me in the secret place. I decree I will not remain where I am but will continue to chase after Him with radical abandonment.

CHAPTER 2

POSITIONED TO HEAR

GOT YOUR COFFEE?

So, there I was on a journey with Jesus, feeling like every day I was going to spontaneously combust because of the excitement that was building in me that Jesus still speaks today. He is not far away, He's not distant, He's not one we must convince to speak to us. He's the God who "leans in." He is the God who "bends down." He is the ever-present God (see Ps. 46:1)—our help, our source, our Lord, Immanuel, *"God with us." "But God demonstrates His own love for us in this: While we were still sinners, Christ died for us"* (Rom. 5:8 NIV). *The Passion Translation* says it this way: *"But Christ proved God's passionate love for us by dying in our place while we were still lost and ungodly!"*

Our relational, loving Jesus! Our beautiful God who so desperately wanted to bridge the great sin divide to return to a relationship with mankind that He sent His one and only Son (see John 3:16). The same God who made a way when there was no way for mankind is the same God who desperately longs and yearns to speak to me, who loves our coffees together more than I do. No matter what anyone said to me, nobody could steal or dampen the fire in me. He is the God who wants deep relationship with me and to teach me to live in the reality that is based simply upon what He speaks and His Word.

As a young girl, I would sit down in front of the television when the station would air *The Ten Commandments* and I would watch Moses interacting with God. I remember the scene of his encounter with the Lord at the burning bush, and it would always impact me so deeply. My heart would be almost beating out of my chest as it cried out, *"I want that! I want to see You like that! I want to hear You like that! That's the type of relationship I want with You! So close! So intimate! So real! So personal! So deep!"*

I literally lived and breathed every day to encounter His heart and hear His voice. Day in and day out, I sought Him from a place of such desperation that I would cry, *"God, I feel like I'm going to die if I don't hear You speak."* I had this exploding, I-feel-like-I-am-going-to-spontaneously-combust hunger to hear from Him. I knew the promise, *"My own sheep will hear my voice and I know each one, and they will follow me"* (John 10:27), but I wanted to explore *the ways* that He speaks.

I read books like *The Final Quest* by Rick Joyner, *The Secret Place* by Dale A. Fife, and *Hearing God's Voice* by Joyce Meyer. As I read page after page, I cried out, *"Jesus, I want encounters like they have. I want to hear like they hear."* I came to find out that I have a journey completely different from these amazing men and women of God. Yes, there is a biblical basis for the ways God speaks, but ever so gently the Lord began to show me that I could not strive to hear as someone else hears. The testimony of others should only *increase my hunger and surrender to His process* of allowing the Holy Spirit to teach me to hear His voice.

For me, that's what happened! In those early years of discovery, the Holy Spirit was my teacher. I am a huge advocate of church community, accountability, and having covering and not being a lone ranger. However, even though I was deeply connected in a church community, for quite a few years of my journey my only teacher was the Holy Spirit. I began to hear from Him in ways that didn't fit in the church culture that I was based in. For years, I would cry out to the Lord for a mentor, but in those forming years He wanted to be my mentor. Later on, He brought the right people at the right time to help me grow and understand more of the gift of prophecy, the office of a prophet, and what I was called to.

My testimony is very much "I learned on the job and I learned as I went." I had very bizarre experiences in my journey of hearing from God, which led me to think that there was something significantly wrong with me. Well, let's be real—I thought I was possessed by a demon! I went to a few churches and asked people to pray for me to "cast out" whatever was in me that was causing these bizarre experiences because they were *so* out of my comfort zone or my "box" of theology.

Many things began to happen that I could not explain. Let's start with the first one that for a Baptist girl was very wild.

I was working for a wonderful church as part of a wonderful team and was learning so much every week about leadership skills and how to train others. Yet even in the midst of this amazing place—being mentored, trained, and equipped by such valuable and amazing people at times I felt like a square peg in a round hole. Why? Because I had a hunger to see the supernatural, angels, dreams, visions, encounters with God, prophetic experiences—things that I had read in Rick Joyner's and Graham Cooke's books.

AN ENCOUNTER THAT CHANGED MY LIFE

One morning, I was in the midst of an "I feel like I am going to spontaneously combust" moment. My hunger was increasing so dramatically. I sat down in my office to go through my "to do" list for the day, and as usual I began my day with the same question: "What is on Your heart today, Jesus? Speak to me, Lord, I am listening!"

Before I could even get *listening* out of my mouth, this overwhelming sensation came over my entire body. The only way I could describe it was a feeling of electricity running through every part of my body. I then heard the same thing that I had heard as a "very strong thought" in one of my first coffee dates with Jesus: *"Pick up your pen and write."* But this time, it was an audible voice. I now understand why mountains tremble at the voice of the Lord.

I was sobbing and shaking like a leaf in my office—not out of fear, but sobbing as my heart cried out, *"Oh my gosh, He's here! He's here!"* My brain couldn't understand it, but my spirit knew He had just walked into the room.

I picked up my pen, like last time over my coffees with Jesus, but this time was completely different. What I now understand to be the power of God and the supernatural empowerment of His Spirit hit my hand. I began to write faster than I have ever written in my entire life. Line after line, the page filled with this beautiful letter from the Lord to me (or so I thought!), and it was all based around encouragement. *"Do not give up! These are the plans that I have for you! You have a great destiny, a great calling."*

Within a few minutes, it was done. The electricity feeling going through my entire body stopped; I fell back in my chair and sobbed some more. I read line after line of His beautiful promises while wanting to run to the window of my office and open it wide and shout from the rooftops, *"He just showed up! I just encountered Him in a way I've never experienced."* I wanted to run and tell everyone who breathed what just happened. In my moment of absolute joy, I heard His audible voice again. This time, He told me to pick up the piece of paper that was filled with such amazing promises, and He told me to go and give it to one of the other pastors.

My heart sank! "But isn't this *my* letter? God...ummmmm...I don't know what I am doing. What in the world am I going to say?" Thoughts bombarded me: "What is he going to say? He is going to think I'm crazy." Remember, I was in a church culture that didn't teach about experiences like this.

Let me tell you, if you looked in the window of my office that morning, you would have seen me pacing back and forth, arms flying everywhere as I tried to convince God that this probably wasn't the greatest of ideas.

I love how He patiently waits! He just sits, loves, encourages, and empowers us with grace in our process. He doesn't bang me over the head with a stick and tell me to get my act together; He journeys with me in my process of obedience, and the hope and prayer is that during our lives we become quicker and quicker at obeying.

So I wrestled and wrestled and eventually I came to a place where a question rose from my heart: *"Can I leave this office today and live with wondering what would have happened if I did what*

God asked?" That was the clincher! I'd rather take the letter next door and maybe fall flat on my face and look silly than not obey what He was asking me to do.

So with knees knocking I went and knocked on his door. I swear it sounded like I was speaking in tongues trying to get my words out to explain what just happened. "I asked God the same question I ask Him every day...then came the electricity feeling, oh hang on, no, I think it was 'pick up your pen and write' first, it was loud, and I cried and I shook and I am not even sure what I'm talking about but I can't shake the feeling I am meant to give this letter to you. God bless you."

And I ran out of that office as fast as I could.

I ran into my office, fell into my chair, and closed the door, breathing heavily. Fear and a sigh of relief that I had obeyed were booming through my heart at the same time. I plonked my head on my desk with a gazillion thoughts going through my mind—what had I just done, what would happen from here, and what if I got it wrong?

Suddenly, sigh of relief and panic attack was interrupted by there was a knock at the door. I mumbled, "Come in," and in came the pastor. My heart sank to the floor. This was the moment of truth! I looked at his eyes, and that's when I noticed his tears. He sat with me and wept and shared with me how that very morning he had gone down into the men's bathroom and told the Lord he couldn't do this anymore. The call was so hard and he was so discouraged, crying out to the Lord to hear him, ready to give up. Then a few hours later, there was a knock on his door. It may have been a knock on the door in the natural, but really it was a knock from heaven to his hurting and discouraged heart. It was a mail delivery from the heart of the Father straight to his heart. I remember so vividly how he looked at me and said, *"Every line on this page is the answer to everything I prayed about."*

That encounter I know marked his life, and it certainly changed mine. That's the God we serve! His voice marks us, changes us, leaves us never the same. That was the defining moment that changed my life forever. It awakened me in even deeper ways to the truth and reality that He still speaks today, He wants to speak to me, but He also wants to speak *through* me to encourage and edify others.

HE STILL SPEAKS!

So began my journey of exploring the ways He speaks, how to partner with Him, and how to steward that prophetic ear muscle. (We will specifically look at this more in depth in Chapter 8.) Just when I thought my socks had been blown off, I was about to move into a reality where I would be living in that place continually. I entered the land of wide-eyed wonder of who He is, how He speaks, His creativity, and the language of the Spirit in ways I'd never dreamed were possible for me.

The tipping point was tipped! It began—but different from how I expected.

It was like a switch got flicked, and things began to change quite rapidly. It was one of those moments when you feel like you have been sowing for so long, doing the groundwork, and then suddenly the breakthrough arrives. I began to notice things start to radically change. I felt I had finally entered a whole new level of experiencing God and hearing His voice. I began to dive even deeper into the Word to really seek out the way that the Lord speaks, to help me understand what I was experiencing.

This is what I learned about ways He can speak:

1. He will always speak through His Word. He will never contradict Himself.

2. He can appear before us like He did in Acts 9.

3. He can speak in an audible voice as He did in First Samuel.

4. He speaks in the still small voice—an internal voice into our hearts and into our minds.

5. The beauty of creation testifies to God Himself (see Rom. 1:19-20).

6. Visions and dreams (see Num. 12:6; Acts 22:17-18).

7. He can speak through impressions or through a knowing (see Neh. 7:5).

8. He also speaks through symbols, signs, newspaper headlines, movies, songs, circumstances, and books.

As I dove into really studying the ways He speaks, the one thing that continued to burn in me was to position myself in such a way that I was living sensitive to His Spirit. I wanted to be one who had eyes to see and ears to hear (see Rev. 3:22, Matt. 13:16). I was so challenged by the creative ways that He can speak, and I wanted to cultivate my heart in the secret place to be open to Him in whatever way He chose to speak. I never wanted to "miss" what He was saying.

So from this point on, the Holy Spirit began to train me in greater ways to hear His voice and *know* it was His voice in ways I wasn't used to. Life dramatically changed as my usual daily routine started getting interrupted by an internal whisper. It would stop me in my tracks and then floor me when the whisper was confirmed.

What do I mean by this? Well, I would be minding my own business shopping when I would hear an internal whisper that told me that when I walked out of the shop and up the street and turned left, I would see a friend of mine, and this "whisper" named my friend. I stopped in my tracks because this whisper was so strong yet so gentle and left my mind doing somersaults trying to figure out what I just heard. I didn't have plans to see this friend on that day—*what is that voice, that whisper? Is that God speaking? But why would He tell me I am about to see a friend when I turn left up the street? Was it audible? Was it a thought? Am I possessed? What's happening to me?* I have a tendency to overthink, and it's something that I have worked hard on, but at this particular time in my life I was still trying to analyze and work out what it was that I just heard.

In any other time in my life, I would have shrugged it off and thought "That's weird!" But in this season, I was so hungry to hear from God that the thought boomed in my heart: "*What if* it's God speaking?"

I finished my shopping and walked up the street. I was walking up the hill, and I could see the corner of the street. I was about to turn left; my heart was beating through my chest. The deciding moment—I turned the corner and straight in front of me a little way up was my friend. In that moment I didn't know whether to start jumping up and down in the middle of the footpath scream-ing, "*I think God just spoke to me,*" or run up to my friend jumping up and down trying to explain what just happened without sound-ing like I was crazy.

Yet in the midst of the excitement, there was still this fear that rumbled around inside of me. *What if this isn't God speaking? What if it's the enemy?* There wasn't any significant encounter that took place—no angels showed up on the scene, no miracle took place, I was just given information about something before it happened. Little did I know that this was going to become the norm for me.

I started to experience this "whisper" more and more. I would be sitting in my living room (before I had a mobile phone) and the house phone would ring. From across the room I would hear this whisper: "Lana, it's your mum," and I would pick up the phone and be greeted with my mum's voice.

Time after time I would be met with this whisper that would give me the "heads-p" on things before they took place. Somewhere along the journey, the fear started to increase more and more. *What if it's not God? What if the next time I hear something it will be bad?* I really started to get myself tied up in knots over it rather than seeing it for what it really was. Rather than enjoying what God was building in me, my mind joined the party, and fear started to hinder the journey.

In the midst of this whirlwind that I found myself in, I was attending Bible college, and I started learning about the gift of prophecy and more and more about how God speaks. This was giving me a "grid" for encounters that I was having with the Lord as I started to learn about the prophetic. So on one hand I was being filled with all this glorious truth about the prophetic, yet on the other hand I was being told something completely different.

I started to share my journey with some people who thought that maybe I needed some type of deliverance ministry; maybe something had opened doors in my life for the enemy to come in and begin to speak to me like this. They felt that I was moving into a realm of almost fortune-telling. This was where the enemy got me tied in knots, because I didn't know what was really happening.

THANK GOD FOR THE ELI'S

God was *training me* to hear His voice. Even before I knew that I would be a prophet to the nations, He was growing me in my prophetic gifting and in the area of foretelling. But the enemy took the truth and twisted it to cause me great anxiety that I had somehow left a door open in my generational line that was now leading me into a realm of fortune-telling. Hindsight is a beautiful thing, isn't it? But at the time, I was a whirlwind of confusion, and the feeling of "not fitting in" was getting stronger as what I was experiencing was so out of the norm with most circles I was moving in, except for the Bible college I had started attending.

My grandfather had dabbled in palm reading and tarot cards for a while, but I had dealt with that stuff in my generational line. Still, the question had been sowed in my heart, and now I just wasn't sure. Confusion had set in. The more I prayed about this, the more I heard this whisper.

In my desire to learn more about hearing from God, I booked myself into a conference that Graham Cooke was speaking at, after hearing so much about his ministry. So off I went to the conference, realizing that this could be a place where I could speak to the pastor and tell him about this "whisper" thing and get him to pray for me and maybe help me navigate what was happening.

I attended the conference, and at the end of a session I went up and spoke to the pastor. I attempted to explain my journey, tripping over all my words. It went something like this: "I hear this whisper; it tells me what's about to happen before it happens. It's happened to me regarding friends I will see before I see them, and then mum was thrown in there somewhere. I think the phone rang and I knew it would be her, and my granddad dabbled in the occult, tarot cards, palm reading—I thought I'd dealt with it, but maybe I haven't? Am I possessed? Are demons talking to me? Am I deceived? Please pray for me quickly, I'm panicking and don't know what to do and people think I'm crazy! Help! Pray, pray, pray right now...*please!*"

I remember the way he looked at me with such compassion and love, and he said to me so calmly, "Have you dealt with your generational stuff regarding your grandfather?"

"Yes, I have had lots of prayer ministry regarding this."

He smiled and said to me, "Well, I'd say then that the Lord is training you to hear His voice; keep asking Him to speak."

Instantly, a peace came over me like a blanket, and it was like I could breathe again. Something was ignited in me that night—something so deep that gave me the permission to celebrate what God was doing in me.

I felt like Samuel, who was sleeping when he heard someone call his name.

> *Then the Lord called Samuel. Samuel answered, "Here I am." And he ran to Eli and said, "Here I am; you called me." But Eli said, "I did not call; go back and lie down." So he went and lay down. Again the Lord called, "Samuel!" And Samuel got up and went to Eli and said, "Here I am; you called me." "My son," Eli said, "I did not call; go back and lie down." Now Samuel did not yet know the Lord: The word of the Lord had not yet been revealed to him. A third time the Lord called, "Samuel!" And Samuel got up and went to Eli and said, "Here I am; you called me." Then Eli*

realized that the Lord was calling the boy. So Eli
told Samuel, "Go and lie down, and if he calls you,
say, 'Speak, Lord, for your servant is listening.'" So
Samuel went and lay down in his place. The Lord
came and stood there, calling as at the other times,
"Samuel! Samuel!" Then Samuel said, "Speak, for
your servant is listening" (1 Samuel 3:4-10 NIV).

I love this demonstration of how the Lord interrupted Samuel's life with His voice, awakening Samuel to a whole new realm of encountering God. For me, I wasn't hearing an "audible" voice, but the whisper was so loud within me it may as well have been audible. And here I was running around trying to work out what was going on until I found an Eli who told me, "I think it's God, ask Him to keep speaking."

So I did. "Here I am, Lord, Your servant is listening."

This built another level of confidence into my heart that God was speaking. The experience also showed me just how much fear can be based around hearing from God. But God is a God who is passionately in love with us and wanting to communicate with us. He is the God who will speak to us in ways that we haven't ever thought of or experienced. Rather than freaking out, we must respond like Samuel: "Lord, is that You? Here I am; Your servant is listening."

Through that experience, God began to train me in a new way. God's heart was for me to be filled with joy in the journey, not fear and panic. It was an invitation to experience Him speaking in a new way. It's important to find the Eli's in our lives who are further along the journey than we are—who have the wisdom and discernment to help position us to go deeper and give us greater clarity.

You may have an Eli who shows up to help you for only one step of your journey, or you may have an Eli who walks with you all the way through your journey, but I want you to hear this. The Lord will bring the right people at the right time to help you along in your journey.

That one experience with my "Eli" shifted things so dramatically for me that I was catapulted into some of the greatest visions and encounters of my life with God. It opened up more and more ways the Lord speaks. I had overcome my first "crisis" of hearing from God—my panic moment when I almost ran away because I thought I was being deceived.

Fear and anxiety will rob your joy, your peace, your intimacy with Jesus. That's exactly what happened to me in this moment of crisis. But I had breakthrough, and I was repositioned and ready for more. My joy and excitement returned—I was actually walking in my breakthrough, hearing from Him more and more, and excited for what He was going to do! He wooed me back to that secret place to be with Him.

So I had experienced the electricity in my hands and writing so fast I could not keep up. I was just beginning to understand the "whisper," the "internal knowing," the "sense"—a small, minute part of how He can train us in the foretelling way He speaks. I was excited for my understanding of how He speaks to grow, and then He opened up another beautiful way that He speaks.

I was in worship day after day, lost in His presence, weeping, undone all over again by His love—and suddenly I was surprised by what took place.

A vision opened up in front of my eyes. I could see it so clearly, so real. I knew at the same time I was right there.

I was in a room, the walls covered in every colored jewel I have ever seen or imagined. Wall after wall was showered with these beautiful gemstones, and there were ladders everywhere to take you up higher into different levels and different rooms. I could hardly believe what I was experiencing, when suddenly that internal whisper came back and whispered to me, "Welcome to the heavenly places!"

Life was changed from this point on.

See you in Chapter Three!

PRAYER

Lord, thank You that You still speak today. Thank You, Lord, for the promise that I can hear Your voice. Thank You that You love to speak to me and that You are always speaking. Lord, continue to train me to hear Your voice, to be sensitive to Your Spirit and how You are speaking to me. Lord, by Your Spirit continue to create in me a hunger to hear Your voice and recognize when You speak. In Jesus's name, amen.

DECREE

Here I am, Lord! I'm listening! I am available! I decree in Jesus's name that I am positioned to hear, and I decree that as I continue to encounter You and Your heart I begin to hear and see more clearly.

CHAPTER 3

The Language of the Spirit

THE WALLS WERE FULL OF JEWELS, EVERY COLOR OF THE rainbow, and it was as if every single jewel screamed *life!* They were so alive, and the atmosphere was full of life like I had never experienced on earth. It was like everything screamed, *"Praise God! Praise Jesus!"* I remember in this vision experiencing a level of joy and peace that I had never known on earth. I remember climbing the ladders, running my hands along the walls of jewels, and the feeling exploding within me, "This is where I was created to be"— the feeling of home.

Then, I saw Jesus. We went up a ladder and into another room, but this room looked like the throne room of God. There were jewels all over the walls again. Such life and beauty, such love, and the feeling of majesty reverberated like sound waves through the atmosphere, like rainbow colors everywhere. My heart was soaring—so happy, so free, a joy I had never known. It reminded me of when John described the glory and the rainbow colors that surround the throne of God like emerald (see Rev. 4:3).

In that moment, Jesus began to speak to the very core of me about who I was. His words poured over me like liquid honey. He spoke things into my heart that were so deep, so beautiful, all around my *true* identity. It wasn't "This is what I want you to do" or "This is who I want you to become." It was all about "This is *who you are.*" As He spoke, His words exploded such truth, such freedom; change was taking place within me. Deep delight filled me as He spoke to the core of my identity.

After that life-changing encounter with Jesus, I had such a deep longing in my heart to go back to that place. What I had seen, what I had experienced was so glorious, I grieved being back in this "normal" reality. That encounter was one of a few that was a marker moment for me because it taught me so much about the way God speaks.

WHEN HE SPEAKS, THINGS CHANGE

Whether we see it with our natural eyes or not, when He speaks, things change!

When He speaks, He creates!

When He speaks, He shifts things!

When He speaks, He aligns things!

When He speaks, He corrects things!

When He speaks, we are invited and drawn into that deeper place of intimacy with Him!

But you know what struck me the most?

When He speaks, He reveals *more of who He is!*

When He speaks, He reveals more of His glorious nature. When He speaks, He reveals more of His glorious goodness. When He speaks, He reveals another facet of who He is.

HIS WORD IS THE BEST BREAD

In Matthew 4:4 Jesus tell us,

> *Bread alone will not satisfy, but true life is found in **every word**, which constantly goes forth from God's mouth.*

The commentary notes in *The Passion Translation* say, "The Aramaic is 'Bar-nasha' and can be translated 'The Son of Man will not live by bread alone.' ...The verb tense implies that man lives not only by the words God has spoken, but also by the words he is speaking. It must be the living Word, not the dead letters that gives us life."[1]

If the Son of Man will not live by bread alone, if Jesus Himself when He walked upon this earth as fully man and fully God did not live by bread alone, how much more do we as God's people need to live in a place where we are feasting upon every word that flows from His mouth every day?

> *Jesus often withdrew to lonely places and prayed* (Luke 5:16 NIV).

So in my position of "withdrawing often," I found myself in that encounter in the heavenly places. This tore open a whole new level of understanding. The Lord speaks through visions and encounters, but His greatest desire when He speaks is to reveal His nature and His heart to us.

It has now been 20 years since my journey of hearing from God began, and that is the most important thing I have learned. He can speak in dreams, visions, through the Word, impressions, movies, books. But whatever "form" He chooses to communicate to His people, all of it is simply another expression of His heart and desire for relationship.

God isn't looking for those who "know it all." (Lord have mercy on us if we ever get to a place where we think we have it all worked out.) He's looking for those who are laid-down lovers and want to grow in relationship with Him. He wants those who have eyes to see and ears to hear Him speaking, those who are falling more in love with Him every time He speaks.

Of course, there are times when God speaks and we are challenged and convicted. He is a good and perfect Father who disciplines His children. But when He corrects us it is *never* to condemn but always to encourage, always to lift us up higher, always to take us from glory to glory (see 2 Cor. 3:18). Even when the Lord speaks to convict and correct, He does it out of His pure heart of love that says, "I love you too much to leave you where you are. You are so much better than this. This isn't who you are; come up higher."

God will never speak to you in a way that brings condemnation. He will never speak to you in a way that tears you down. When He speaks to you, His intention and aim is to reveal something more to you about who He is and His ways so that you will look more like Him.

> *Now it's time to be made new by every revelation that's been given to you. And to be transformed as you embrace the glorious Christ-within as your new life and live in union with him!* (Ephesians 4:23-24)

So again—when He speaks, things change!

When He speaks, He creates!

When He speaks, He shifts things!

When He speaks, He aligns things!

When He speaks, He corrects things!

When He speaks, He heals!

When He speaks, He delivers!

When He speaks, He ignites!

When He speaks, He refreshes!

When He speaks, He rejuvenates!

When He speaks, He causes the dead places to spring to life again!

I want you to hear this—*you were created with the ability to hear from Him!*

Every day of your life and your journey with Him, He wants to open up more and more to you the beautiful realm of how He speaks. You and I will forever be learning to understand His supernatural language.

When Jesus spoke to His disciples, He often spoke in parables because they were an invitation to "search Him out." The mysteries of the Kingdom are communicated in a language that is so different from ours.

> *It is God's privilege to conceal things and the king's*
> *privilege to discover them* (Proverbs 25:2 NLT).

I love what Bill Johnson says: "God doesn't hide things *from* you; He hides them *for* you." He wants to be searched out. He wants to be pursued. In the process of searching Him out and searching out

41

the hidden things, you find *treasure*. In fact, you find *the* greatest treasure—you find out more about who He is.

My greatest joy in my journey of hearing from God, especially in these latter years, has been the *joy* that it is to go on a "treasure hunt" with Jesus. To find that place of such deep intimacy with Him that He shares the secrets of His heart with us. That, by far, is still the greatest pleasure and privilege of my life—to be invited into what is in His heart and what He is creating with what He is speaking. As He created the world by His Word in Genesis 1, so He has invited you and me into that place to partner with Him in what He is creating in us, for us, and through us by His Word.

God has so much He wants to reveal to you and speak to you. It's just a matter of learning to have your ears "tuned to the right station." We cannot allow the moments of "static" when we can't hear clearly to deter us from the glorious journey of learning to hear His voice.

On my journey of hearing from God, I have seen God speak in ways I would never have imagined. We cannot squeeze God into a box of how *we think* He should speak to us. We must be open with eyes to see and ears to hear when He turns up and starts to speak in ways we don't expect.

I have many stories of how the Lord has begun to speak in unexpected ways. Let me begin by telling you one of my favorites that taught me one of the greatest keys to understand how He is speaking.

PAY ATTENTION TO REPETITION

As I shared in the beginning of this book, a key to hearing from God is expecting Him to speak to you, asking Him to open your eyes to see and hear what He's saying, and looking for Him everywhere. You want to live in that place of intentionality, looking for Him at the supermarket, the library, the coffee shop, everywhere you go—always asking Him to show you how He's speaking.

So I began to live my life with greater intentionality, looking for Him, and I started to notice a certain symbol appearing almost daily. Do you know what symbol that was? It was the Eiffel Tower.

I would walk into a clothing store and see an Eiffel Tower on a shirt in front of me; I would watch a movie and the Eiffel Tower would appear; I would open up a book and see the Eiffel Tower on the pages. People would walk past me with Eiffel Towers on their shirts; people would start giving me gifts of Eiffel Towers.

After a few weeks of being bombarded with the same symbol over and over, I began to think, "Is God speaking to me?" I don't believe in coincidences with the Holy Spirit; I believe in God-incidences. He wants to speak to us more than we desire to hear, and we *must* have confidence that when He speaks He confirms His word.

> *I will make sure that by the testimony of two or three witnesses every matter will be confirmed* (2 Corinthians 13:1).

He will confirm it two or three times and then it is established (see Deut. 19:15 NIV).

It's normal to wonder, "What if I'm being deceived? What if I miss it?" But we can't live focused on that fear, or we may find ourselves in a place of "static," where it's harder and harder to hear from Him. Instead, we need to put our faith in the One who can keep us and confirm His Word to us.

With this repetition of the Eiffel Tower, I felt this stirring excitement in me. Instead of "What if I am being deceived?" "What if I am missing it?" I thought, "What about the other side of the coin? What if it's God?" So I began to activate my faith, praying, *"God, if this is You, I am listening; please open this up to me more. Give me eyes to see and wisdom and understanding."*

The weeks went on, the Eiffel Towers continued to appear everywhere, and the question arose: *"What are You saying, Lord?"* One day, a sense filled me so intensely to research the history of the Eiffel Tower and what it represents.

I began to read and research and found out that the Eiffel Tower was used as a communications tower in World War I to call people to the front lines. It is based in the city of love, Paris, and within it is an elevator to take people higher. From the top, they can see the view of all of Paris. As I began to read these facts, the Lord started to speak to me.

"Lana, the Eiffel Tower is a representation of what I have called you to. I have called you to hear the messages of My heart, the sound waves of heaven, to release My broadcast. To see people more deeply rooted and grounded in intimacy with Me—the divine romance, the lover of their souls—and in the revelation of My love and My Word. From that place, people will be awakened to their authority, their position in Me, and learn to live from a higher perspective, to see as I see."

KEYS TO UNDERSTANDING THE CREATIVE WAYS HE SPEAKS

I was blown out of the water by His creativity in how He speaks. The Lord taught me three very important lessons through that experience:

1. Pay attention to repetition: Whether it is a Scripture you see over and over, a symbol, a sentence, a word, a name—whatever it is, pay attention to the repetition.

2. Ask the Lord for the Spirit of revelation and wisdom.

   My heart is always full and overflowing with thanks to God for you as I constantly remember you in my prayers. I pray that the Father of glory, the God of our Lord Jesus Christ, would impart to you the riches of the Spirit of wisdom and the Spirit of revelation to know him through your deepening intimacy with him (Ephesians 1:16-17).

3. Research: If the Lord is highlighting a symbol, a sentence, picture, or a word, I always want to place value upon what He is speaking, so I will do what I can do by researching in the natural what that symbol, saying, sentence, word, or name means.

So much revelation that I have received over the years has come from researching and studying what the Lord is highlighting.

NUMBERS, NUMBERS, EVERYWHERE

As my journey progressed with the Lord and I *paid attention to repetition*, I started to notice something very bizarre. I would look at the clock in the morning and it was 11:11. A minute later

I would walk into the kitchen and the microwave time was not right—it would say 11:11. I would go to bed at night, and I would lie in bed and grab my phone to turn my alarm on for the next morning and it would be 11:11. I would be watching movies, and the time on the screen in the movie was 11:11.

This went on for weeks and weeks and weeks. I had no idea what was going on, except that again before me was another series of *repetitions*. So I began to ask the Lord to give me wisdom and revelation, and I began to study the number eleven in Scripture.

My experience up until this point was that the most common way God speaks is through His Word; He speaks in that inner voice through our reading, meditating upon the Word, and through our prayer life. So starting to see numbers appearing everywhere was very much outside of my history and experience with God's voice. I am not saying this is the way God will speak to you; this is just one of my experiences, and I am *not* endorsing numerology. I have never been part of it, and I would never encourage any believer to enter into it. But I knew in this repetition that God was speaking to me again in a creative way.

I knew numbers were significant for the Lord. In Scripture, He didn't just choose "forty days" or "walk around Jericho for seven days" just because He felt like throwing those numbers in there for no reason. There was a significance, there was a message, there was a strategy.

So in my 11:11 journey, I knew the Lord was speaking in these numbers because of the sudden repetition. But you know what happened? Nothing!

I cried out; I asked the Lord every time it would appear or I would see it. I so longed to know what it meant, but I had no idea.

I began to get frustrated in the waiting and the not knowing. I felt that niggle of fear try to creep in again: *"You're missing what He's saying. Maybe you're being deceived."*

The waiting began to frustrate me. I began to feel discouraged. We live in a society and culture that wants things quickly, and I wanted an instant answer, but God wanted to ignite hunger in me and teach me something in the waiting. You know what He taught me? He taught me that every little moment of repetition, every time I saw 11:11 and I knew that He was speaking, that was a moment when He was invading my world. That was a moment when He was whispering to me, *"I'm here."* The feeling of God showing up in the middle of my day in little fun ways began to shift my heart from being discouraged that I had no idea what He was saying, to being excited. Every time I saw 11:11, it put a massive smile on my face that made my heart sing, "Oh, *hi Lord!*" Knowing He was speaking to me in every little 11:11 moment ignited my heart with a flutter of joy that He was so intimately involved in my day and created a hunger in me to know Him more than I ever had.

I know that God confirms His word out of the mouths of two or three witnesses, so I just had to activate my faith in the waiting, stay positioned, keep asking, and every time the 11:11 would appear, I would ask the Lord again.

One Sunday, I was sitting in a service at Glory City Church in Brisbane, Australia, and my beautiful friend Katherine Ruonala got up on the platform and began to share that she was seeing 11:11 everywhere and had begun seeking the Lord for its meaning. I almost fell off my chair again! A lot of my relationship with God consists of me almost or often falling off my chair in awe of His creative language, confirmation, and how He speaks.

I was on the edge of my chair with bated breath, waiting for those next glorious words of revelation to pour forth out of her mouth. She went on to share that when she asked the Lord about 11:11, He spoke to her and led her to John 11:11. After that time, Jeff Jansen ministered at Glory City Church and he mentioned in passing about 11:11, with reference to John 11:11 and other revelations the Lord had shared with him. That was a great, comforting confirmation to Katherine. God confirmed His word of the season of John 11:11.

> *Then Jesus added, "Lazarus, our friend, has just fallen asleep. It's time that I go and awaken him"* (John 11:11).

The season of awakening! My heart was so full of joy. I realized that the Lord was not only speaking to me about the dry and dead places in my life that were about to be awakened by the resurrection power of Jesus, but it was also a word for the body of Christ.

God speaks in *many* ways, as we are discovering together through this book, but when you start seeing repetition—pay attention and don't fear! God will confirm what He is saying. I *love* that the Lord never goes outside of His Word, and He speaks and backs up what He is saying with Scripture. For me, a major "word girl," I love that! How out of the box He can speak and then give you the answer and revelation using the Word.

I love it!

POPCORN IS POPPING EVERYWHERE

Another time, I was sitting with the Lord having a cup of coffee, and the Lord asked me a question. "Lana, do you know what season it is?"

I replied, "Ummm, no, Lord, I don't."

His reply almost knocked me off my chair (again). He said, "It is the season of *popcorn!*"

Now this was a stretch for me. What in the world has popcorn got to do with anything? There isn't any reference to popcorn in Scripture!

In this moment, my mind and soul were screaming *"Rebuke it!"* It didn't fit into my box of understanding. So I tried to push it aside and press deeper into worship, convincing myself that it was my mind taking me in weird directions, until the words came again: *"Popcorn! Popcorn!"* This time the sense was so strong, I knew it was the Lord; even though my mind didn't understand, my spirit knew it was God.

So I humbly confessed to the Lord my lack of understanding and asked the Lord to please explain it to me.

Sometimes God will speak in a way that offends our minds to reveal our hearts, and this revealed some "boxes" in my heart where my understanding of how creatively He speaks needed to expand a little more.

"So here I am, Lord. Please explain to me what You mean by popcorn."

Instantly, I got the understanding like a flood, and my hand began to write at a thousand miles an hour. I had a vision—the Lord showed me that I and God's people had been sowing seeds faithfully, over and over, despite hardship and pressure, and now there was going to be sudden accelerated breakthrough.

I was *so* encouraged how the Lord could speak *so* creatively. Yet again, the Lord had spoken so clearly through a symbol of these seeds that I had been sowing in my faith, declarations, prayers, and obedience. Fiery trials had come against me to try to discourage me that God's promises in my life weren't going to come to pass, but now the fire of His love was going to fall upon my life in such a profound way that I would be undone again by His love. Not only that, but all those seeds were going to start popping in break-through and manifestation, and my contending season was going to be a testimony carrying the fragrance of Jesus and His goodness, kindness, and love to draw others to Himself, to taste and see that He is good (see Ps. 34:8).

After that encounter with the Lord I found myself hearing the Lord whisper as I ministered the Lord whispered to me to share the *popcorn story* and to decree breakthrough over the congregation. I was wrestling, but I felt the Lord's prompting. I released the prophetic word, and people shouted with excitement and loud amens at the word the Lord had released.

From that point on, I would have person after person approach me to sharee their stories of dreams about popcorn, unusual cravings for popcorn, and not even liking popcorn but having a strong urge to eat it lately. These people were hearing the Lord speaking to them through the symbol of popcorn in their prayer time. One after another, I was approached by people to whom the Lord had confirmed His Word, a message for the season.

All throughout that ministry tour, everywhere I went I saw *popcorn*. Boxes of *popcorn* were left on my bed in hotel rooms in beautiful, abundant gift baskets full of food—before the givers had heard my story. It was a shining confirmation of the word of the Lord in a food basket.

God is *fun* and He's *so* creative in how He speaks. We just need to be open, looking, positioned, and expectant for Him to speak. He spoke through a donkey in Numbers 22; He can speak through the most creative and unique ways. We just need to be asking for eyes to see and ears to hear to recognize the language He is using with us all individually.

GOD SPOKE TO YOU THROUGH LICENSE PLATES?

I began noticing repetition of license plates. Week after week, I would be driving and see 555 on license plates continuously. Cars would cut in front of me with 555 on their license plate. Other cars had 202, 666, 777, 222, one after another, all the time. For months on end, there was so much repetition. By this stage, I had grabbed some amazing resources on understanding symbols, dreams, visions, and numbers, such as *The Divinity Code* and *God's Prophetic Symbolism in Everyday Life* by Adam F. Thompson and Adrian Beale and Doug Addison's book *Understand Your Dreams Now*—both wonderful resources on dreams, visions, and symbols. (We will talk more about dreams in another chapter.) I would use those often to help me understand what the Lord was saying. Along with these strong, biblically based resources, I continued to ask the Lord to reveal to me what He was saying.

One day I was driving along with my husband Kevin, and we both saw 202 again and again on license plates. This time it was two cars in two minutes, and we both knew it was the Lord. Instantly, the Lord spoke to me: "Lana, look up Psalm 20:2."

I opened *The Passion Translation* by Dr. Brian Simmons on my phone and I almost cried:

> *May supernatural help be sent from his sanctuary!*
> *May he support you from Zion's fortress!*

What did I need more than ever in that moment and in that season? I needed supernatural help and support to continue to walk through that which the Lord was leading me into. In that season, I was in a deep place of contending, believing God for a breakthrough and for His promises to manifest, and nothing in the natural really looked promising.

Well guess what happened? I started to see the number 666 on license plates *everywhere*. Now, 666 isn't a great number, or so I kept thinking! I would drive along rebuking the devil, and yet I'd hear nothing. There wasn't any revelation coming to me, I couldn't hear the Lord saying anything, but I was certain that 666 wasn't a positive thing, so He was trying to highlight something negative. Confusion swirled around me till I heard a still, small voice inside me.

"Lana, try reading Psalm 66:6."

Ohhhhhhhhhhhh!

I had allowed preconceived ideas and what I knew 666 represented to be my first "port of call" rather than my usual first port of call: "Lord, what are You saying?"

> *He made a highway going right through the Red Sea as the Hebrews passed through on dry ground, exploding with joyous excitement over the miracles of God* (Psalm 66:6).

Exactly what I needed! A word on breakthrough, deliverance, and a miracle! God moved totally outside what I thought I knew. I thought God was saying 666, "rebuke the devil," but really the Lord was saying Psalm 66:6: "You are about to cross over, break through!"

Again, the most common way the Lord speaks is through His Word and the still, small voice we hear in prayer. He speaks through visions and dreams, which we will explore soon, but to say those are the "only way" He speaks would be to limit our understanding of the language of the Holy Spirit. Ask Him to awaken you to the way He speaks through your day-to-day life and the most unexpected things. Lean in and ask Him to give you revelation of what He is saying, eyes to see, and ears to hear. Ask Him to confirm His Word and speak through Scripture. I guarantee you, a whole new level of hearing His voice will open up to you and fill you with the *joy* and *wonder* of who He is.

Why in the world have I shared these stories with you? Because I want to whet your appetite. The way God speaks is so unique, creative, and *fun!* He speaks to us all differently, but it is so important to pay attention to repetition, to research symbols that He highlights, and to ask Him to give you the Spirit of revelation and wisdom. He confirms His word and "winks" His confirmation over what He releases into your life.

Yes, I move in the prophetic office; I am a prophet God uses to speak the times and seasons. God gives me messages and themes for the seasons through different symbols, but He has also spoken to me personally through symbols for my own life. My heart is that these stories would encourage you to look for Him everywhere and that the Holy Spirit would ignite even more hunger within you to look for Him in the Word first, in your prayer life, but also in your everyday life. He may just speak to you through the most bizarre and unexpected of ways.

He spoke to me recently as I was waking up, "I am the God who shows up and speaks in the most unexpected ways!"

PRAYER

Thank You, Lord, for the creative ways that You speak. Holy Spirit, open my spiritual eyes to see more than I have ever seen. Open my ears to hear clearer than I have ever heard. Take me deeper into the revelation of Your Word; I live by every word that flows from Your mouth. Teach me to see You in the unique places, to pay attention to repetition, to look for You everywhere. I invite You, Holy Spirit—come and teach me to be like a child, living in wide-eyed wonder and awe of the creative ways that You speak. In Jesus's name, amen.

DECREE

I live not by bread alone but by every word that flows from the mouth of God. I will not limit the ways the Lord wants to speak; I will look for the creative ways that He is speaking to me. I will pay attention to repetition. I decree a whole new level of joy over my journey of hearing from God in Jesus's name.

NOTE

1. Brian Simmons, Matthew: *Our Loving King* (Racine, WI: BroadStreet Publishing, 2017), 20, footnotes d,e.

CHAPTER 4

DISCERNING THE VOICE: WHAT TO SHARE, WHAT TO HOLD ON TO

I CAMP QUITE A BIT ON PSALM 25:14:

> *There's a private place reserved for the lovers of God,*
> *where they sit near him and receive the revelation-*
> *secrets of his promises.*

We each have a private place with the Lord—that place reserved just for you and Him, that special place. Our secret place. It's the place where He shares His heart; it's the place where He shares the revelation secrets of His promises.

The thing with a "private place" is there's no one else there—it's secluded, it's withdrawn, it's guarded, it's protected, not everyone has free access. You have that special place with the Lord. It's the treasured place, the inner sanctum of the bridal chamber, the deep and beautiful Song of Songs place. No one else can "take your place" reserved for you with Him. Your relationship with Jesus is special, it's unique, it's yours.

You connect with God in your way, and I connect with God in my way. You may connect with God in nature—as soon as you go outside and in you are at the beach or on a mountaintop, you may feel you can hear Him clearer than ever. For me, I turn on worship music and grab my cup of coffee and I am instantly in that place where I can "enter in." The Lord taught me early on to "pay attention" to the places where I connect with His heart and enter into His presence in the easiest way, like I slip right in. Where were those places where I felt close to Him? So I found those places. I found worship and chatting with the Lord over coffee and the Word with my journal are the places where, no matter what's going on in my day or in my heart, if I "pull away" into that place I can enter in. As I "sow" into that place, the worries of the day and the anxieties of my heart fall away.

We are all created to connect with God, and we are all created for relationship with Him. Likewise, my relationship with my husband Kevin is different from my best friend's relationship with her husband. Both of us have deep relationships with our husbands, but they look different and they are meant to.

Your history with the Lord is different from mine. Your encounters and experiences with the Lord are different from mine, and that's good because the Lord doesn't want to encounter us all in the same way. He is a personal God, and over the years I have seen what an amazing God He is in the ways He loves to speak and relate to us as His children. He knows how to speak to us because He knows us so deeply—He created us.

> *You formed my innermost being, shaping my delicate inside and my intricate outside, and wove them all together in my mother's womb. I thank you, God, for making me so mysteriously complex! Everything you do is marvelously breathtaking. It simply amazes me to think about it! How thoroughly you know me, Lord! You even formed every bone in my body when you created me in the secret place, carefully, skillfully shaping me from nothing to something. You saw who you created me to be before I became me! Before I'd ever seen the light of day, the number of days you planned for me were already recorded in your book. Every single moment you are thinking of me! How precious and wonderful to consider that you cherish me constantly in your every thought! O God, your desires toward me are more than the grains of sand on every shore! When I awake each morning, you're still with me* (Psalm 139:13-18).

I wanted to have this verse written out here, rather than just the Scripture reference, because there are a few jewels that I want to share with you that I believe are so life-giving and encouraging.

First, He formed you—He shaped you, He knows you intricately inside and out, and He put you together in your mother's womb. So He knows you pretty well, right? Verse 14 says, "I thank you, God, for making me so mysteriously complex!" Mysteriously complex! You are mysteriously complex and so am I! He knows all of that complexity, so He knows the way to reach you. He knows the way to encounter you! He knows the way to speak to you in your personality, in your makeup, because He made you.

Second, He is always thinking about you! Always!

I want you to hear this—comparison will hinder your relationship with the Lord. It will hinder the way you hear from God. It will hinder the way you connect with Him.

I used to go to conferences as a young girl, and I would sit under Rick Joyner's and Graham Cooke's teaching and I would *long* to have relationships with the Lord like they did. I wanted to hear as they did, I wanted to see as they did, I wanted to know the Lord like they did.

Now there was a healthy part of that—their testimony and life created a hunger in me to know Jesus in the depth of intimacy like they carried. They were carrying something I had yet to experience. They had found a place in the heart of God I hadn't found yet. But I found myself thinking that I needed to hear and see and experience like they did. So I spent a lot of time crying out for a relationship with the Lord like they had. Were dreams, visions, and encounters available to me? Absolutely! But did it have to look like their relationship with God and did I have to have the same experiences as them? No!

What I couldn't put into words at the time, but can now, is that I was so hungry for the "more" of God—to know His heart so deeply and to see the supernatural realm invade my life in greater ways than I had ever imagined. I wanted the truth that the supernatural realm is more real than the natural realm to crash into my life in every way, every day! I wanted to see signs, wonders, and miracles break out all around me as I simply sought His heart. I wanted those moments every day where my breath was taken away because I had encountered His heart or God had showed up.

My problem was I thought it needed to *look* like their relationship. So I laid down comparison. I realized that He knows me so deeply that He knows the way to speak to me, and as Psalm 139:17 says, every moment He is thinking of me and cherishing me in His thoughts. Well, I want to know every moment what those thoughts are. If He is thinking about me every moment, I want to know *what* He is thinking about me and I want to hear it in the way that He wants to speak it to me. I don't want to try to hear or encounter Him in a way that someone else does.

So in my private place with Him, I invited Him to come in and rid my heart of comparison and to remove fear. There is so much fear around hearing from God, which I have talked about in previous chapters. *"What if I hear wrong? What is He going to say to me? How do I know it's God?"* If I entertain those questions, I will be shut down and find it harder to hear from God.

FEAR CANNOT BE THE FULL STOP

So I learned that *fear can't be the full stop*. There can be questions, there can be fear, but we must push past the fear in our journey of hearing from God. Push past the anxieties and know that this is a beautiful relationship, and part of relationship is learning to get to know one another. It's about learning to communicate and understand communication. So in your journey with the Lord and hearing His voice, if you still have those times of fear and anxiety I want to encourage you—give yourself grace. Enjoy your private place with the Lord. Don't try to cultivate your relationship with God to look like someone else's. Don't try to hear from God like someone else. Allow others' testimonies to create a hunger in you for *more*, but don't allow the box to be created that you "must" hear from God the same way.

Invite the Holy Spirit to show you more and more the *way* that you hear from Him, and talk to others in your life about the ways that you experience God and His heart. But whatever way you hear from God—whether you see visions a lot, you dream, you hear audibly, you feel things, you get major revelation from the Word, you have gut feelings—whatever way, don't shut it down because you don't understand it or it doesn't look like someone else's relationship with the Lord. Just enjoy that private place with Him. Just enjoy Him! Minister to Him!

Settle into your sweet spot with Him and enjoy the process of hearing from Him. Don't allow fear and comparison to steal this from you.

SQUARE PEG IN A ROUND HOLE

For so many years of my journey with Jesus and growing in learning to hear from Him, I felt like such a square peg in a round hole. I had wonderful friends who loved the Lord, but my relationship with the Lord was "weird"; it was "different." I was having experiences that they hadn't had and didn't understand, so as much as they loved me and wanted to help me, they didn't know how. So I was always left feeling like I had no idea how to fit in.

I struggled to embrace my relationship with the Lord for what it was. Thoughts plagued me, I felt weird; I compared myself to others and wondered if I should change, but one day something shifted in my heart. My *love* for Jesus and the *joy* I found in my relationship with Him began to outweigh the feeling of comparison or the pressure to "fit in" or make my relationship with the Lord look a certain way.

I was in a beautiful church every week where I had built some amazing friendships. The leadership had helped me so much in developing my leadership skills, and knowledge and revelation of the Word yet they could not help me with my prophetic experiences and encounters. Still, I found that I suddenly felt free in a whole new way to just move in my unique relationship with Jesus.

So on a Sunday night I would be in worship, so overtaken by His presence, so in love with Jesus I could hardly contain it. Everyone around me was worshiping the Lord, but no one raised their hands. I was overtaken with the supernatural joy in my relationship with Jesus; I got so lost in His beauty and presence I just started to raise my hands. I was taken, week after week, into a whole new place with Him, and I would forget my surroundings. The cares of of my relationship having to look like someone else's or needing to hear God like someone else, all fell away. I was just whisked away into this beautiful place with Jesus Sunday after Sunday.

Years later, after I had left that beautiful church, I saw one of the ladies who attended there. We had a lovely conversation, and I was struck by her words: "You know, Lana, I watched you worship week after week after week at church, so in love with Jesus—so much joy, so much hunger, such a depth of relationship with Jesus. Every week I watched you worship, my hunger increased. I cried out 'God whatever it is Lana has, I need that! I want that!'"

I was blown away that without even knowing it my relationship with the Lord was ministering to someone else and igniting hunger within someone else. The Lord was the one who brought that shift within my heart and released so much joy that I chose to no longer be contained by comparison. The joy of my intimacy with Jesus broke the chains of comparison in that area of my life, and I dove right in. Because I embraced the uniqueness of my relationship with Jesus, the Lord used my divine dance of intimacy with Him to minister to someone else.

Isn't that just like Him?

YOUR ANCHOR POINT

That "sweet spot" private place where you connect with Him is your anchor point. No matter what's going on, you can run to that place and connect with Him. When we are trying really hard to see or hear, our striving can often get in the way. You will be surprised how many times the Lord will speak to you as you just position yourself to *enjoy Him* and be with Him.

He wants to share His heart with you more than you want to hear, so I lift off the pressure from you, right now, in Jesus's name. That heavy pressure that you have to get it right, that you have to have the right formula to hear from Him. Just sow, sow, sow, sow in your private place with Him. *Enjoy* Him and let Him teach you, let Him reveal Himself to you.

I have learned that He honors the place where we draw close to be with Him and just enjoy Him, but He also loves to surprise us. He loves to divinely interrupt and show up unexpectedly. He wants to show up "out of the blue—those moments when you are going about your day and suddenly He steps in.

I've had countless encounters with the Lord and moments of deep revelation as I have been chopping veggies in the kitchen preparing dinner or washing dishes. Suddenly, I sense Him so strongly. He's walked into the room. One key for me was cultivating sensitivity.

A lot of my life, my prayer has been for the Lord to create in me a heart that knows when He enters the room before He says a word. A heart that is soft and sensitive to Him and knows His presence so that the moment the atmosphere shifts, I recognize it and stop whatever I am doing because He is here. Don't doubt the power of your prayer for sensitivity. He loves to calibrate and increase sensitivity. He will not turn a deaf ear to a heart cry that is asking for greater sensitivity to His presence. Some of your greatest encounters with the Lord can be while peeling carrots or chopping celery—it is just learning to recognize when He shows up. It's about responding to those moments when He interrupts your day and invites you and calls you to "come away." He is so passionately in love with you—His thoughts toward you are *constant*. He is such a good Father and loves to hang out with you; He will show up out of the blue. We just need to recognize when He does.

TREAT HIS HEART WITH CARE

The Lord loves to share His heart. He is so passionate about relationship. He loves to share what He is thinking about and dreaming about, and part of learning to cultivate our relationship with the Lord and hearing His voice is to *treat His heart with care*.

What do I mean by that? It is an incredible privilege to hear from the Lord, to be invited into the place where the Lord shares what He is thinking about and dreaming about with us, and that is a place we are never to take for granted. Part of stewarding a word from God, which we will look at more in depth in Chapter 8, is to *place value upon* what He is saying. To not "hear what He says" and move on to the next thing, but to be intentional in placing value upon His voice.

Over the years, the Lord has really showed me that privilege in so many ways. I have often had encounters with the Lord where He is longing and looking for those who will treat His heart with care—those who will steward His heart with integrity and purity. Part of that process for me and a valuable part of what the Lord has taught me has been this: *not everything is to be shared.*

Not everything the Lord shares with you is to be shared with others. That's part of your "private place" with the Lord. That is the whole essence of a *secret*—it's not to be told to everyone. There is a very important place we must cultivate in our relationship with the Lord where He knows that He can trust us with what He is sharing. This is why we need to know Him well, know His heartbeat, and ask for greater sensitivity and discernment to know when and what to share and who to share it with. Believe me, I have been on this journey of hearing from God for over 20 years, and I still find myself asking the Lord for greater insight and discernment in this area.

I want to encourage you to ask for discernment with what you feel the Lord is speaking and revealing to you. I am not saying to become a lone ranger and not tell anyone—that's not healthy. We need accountability and we need covering, but we must be asking the Holy Spirit to lead us to those whom you *can* share with. So many times in my earlier years of hearing from God, out of excitement I shared a great revelation that He gave me with someone and ended up with them looking at me like I had two heads. The things God speaks to you, the revelations that He gives you, are precious. They are precious jewels, precious pearls that He gives you from His heart, and we must treat His heart with care and sensitivity regarding what we share and don't share (see Matt. 7:6).

The New International Version of Psalm 25:14 says it this way: *"The Lord confides in those who fear him; he makes his covenant known to them."* Those who fear Him. Those who live in reverence of who He is. Those who live in the wonder of who He is—He *confides* in them. Gosh! What a privilege!

That's a Secret!

God may share secrets with you concerning someone else, someone you know. He may show you something going on in their life, or He may show you an issue they are struggling with. That doesn't necessarily mean that you are to share it with that person. The Lord will often reveal secrets of His heart so we can pray and align with what He wants to do and shift things through our prayers. In our secret, private place, we can partner with Him to turn things around. To decree His heart, to decree breakthrough, to decree life, to decree the answer He is releasing.

Don't rush to release revelation! Whatever secret He shares with you, guard it well. You never know—your prayer, your intercession, your decree could be the breaker anointing that sets someone free, that sees someone saved, that sees someone healed.

Sometimes secrets that He releases are simply for you to *see,* not to *sound aloud!* He invites us into that place of sharing His heart to *see* so we can decree a *shift*. Then, sometimes He shares insights with us that are to be shared.

Uncovering the Plans of the Enemy

In your secret, private place with the Lord, He sometimes shares insights that uncover the plans of the enemy.

His voice uncovers. His voice awakens truth. His voice is always bringing life and alignment. As His children with the ability to hear His voice and live in the depth of relationship where we commune daily with Him, He invites us into the place of divine insight.

The Lord's heart for us is to live in the victory that is already ours. We have eternal victory that is assured through Jesus Christ and the price He paid through His death to reconcile us to the Father. As we say *yes* to Him and surrender our lives, acknowledging Him as Lord and Savior, we step into that assured, eternal victory.

> *But thanks be to God! He gives us the victory through our Lord Jesus Christ* (1 Corinthians 15:57 NIV).

I believe that in our relationship with the Lord, He wants us to be in a place where we are continually hearing His voice and living in victory. That can look like hearing Him give us insight in a "heads-up" so we are one step ahead of the enemy.

What do I mean by this? Let's look at Second Kings 6:8-12:

> *Now the king of Syria was making war against Israel; and he consulted with his servants, saying, "My camp will be in such and such a place." And the man of God sent to the king of Israel, saying, "Beware that you do not pass this place, for the Syrians are coming down there." Then the king of Israel sent someone to the place of which the man of God had told him. Thus he warned him, and he was watchful there, not just once or twice. Therefore the heart of the king of Syria was greatly troubled by this thing; and he called his servants and said to them, "Will you not show me which of us is for the king of Israel?" And one of his servants said, "None, my lord, O king; but Elisha, the prophet who is in*

> *Israel, tells the king of Israel the words that you speak in your bedroom"* (NKJV).

Elisha knew the plans of the king of Syria—the very words that he spoke in his bedroom. Elisha the prophet was given the divine insight from the Lord to know where the king of Syria was setting up his camp. So *every* time, *time* and *time again*, the king of Israel was warned and watchful, and every time the ambush was foiled.

Now, is this a level that a prophet operates in? Absolutely! Is there a significant role that the prophet has in revelation the Lord releases? Absolutely!

> *Surely the Sovereign Lord does nothing without revealing his plan to his servants the prophets* (Amos 3:7 NIV).

But I also believe that there is a place of divine insight that we can live in as believers, close to His heart, where He allows us to see the plans of the enemy so we can be one step ahead. We can hear from the Father that the enemy has set something up for us to "trip." Because of the insight and revelation of the Lord, we bypass that and move forward without hindrance.

Ever had the strongest "gut feeling" to not go somewhere? Or the Lord has told you not to do something? Or you have had a dream, and the Lord has clearly shown you something that would happen if you went down a certain road or a certain pathway? You only find out later what would have happened if you did go down that road or do that thing.

God wants us living so close to His heart that we are living in a place of discernment and hearing His heart. When He reveals a strategy of the enemy, we turn it on its head before it can have a chance to take root.

We have to go to a deeper level of knowing His heart, recognizing His voice, and partnering with Him to overturn the plans of the enemy. The nations and the world need the body of Christ fully awake and living close to His heart, awakened to their authority, to foil the plans of the enemy through the divine insight and strategy that He is releasing.

Yes, Elisha did that for a nation, but what about your family? What about your workplace? What about your sphere of influence?

You have been given that place of influence by the Lord, and as you lean into His heart and continue to journey in hearing His voice, He will speak to you about the glorious things to come and the plans that He has for you. As you pray and seek Him about those areas of your life, He will give you the strategy to foil the enemy's plans when they have taken root and, at times, before they have a chance to. Living awakened to heaven's strategy for our circles of influence is so powerful.

Now hear me—I am not saying go out looking for the enemy or demon behind every tree. I am not saying that. I do not focus on what God isn't doing; I always look for what He is doing. I will not live my life with my head under a rock. We must not be ignorant of the enemy's devices (see 2 Cor. 2:11).

> *Be alert and of sober mind. Your enemy the devil prowls around like a roaring lion looking for someone to devour* (1 Peter 5:8 NIV).

We are moving into a whole new realm of living victorious as the overcoming people of God as we continue to lean into His heart and move in greater discernment and revelation. You and I never know what our prayers shift, what our prayers prevent, what our prayers release.

I live my life every day with, "Lord, what is on Your heart today? What do You want to say today?" From that place, I am *available* for Him to share His heart with me, His secrets, His revelation, His insight, and I can partner with what He is doing on the earth in greater ways.

WHAT IF I DON'T UNDERSTAND THE WARNING I'VE RECEIVED?

So as we have seen, out of His love God will give us warnings or a heads-up. We need to learn to pay attention to those things however they come. That place of greater insight to foil the enemy's plans, shift a circumstance, or partner with the Lord for a turnaround can sometimes get complicated.

You may be asking the question that I have asked a lot in my life: "What if I don't understand the warning I've received or know what to do with it?"

Now for me, I am a times-and-seasons prophet, and I am also a watchman. The Lord has given me eyes to see the strategy of the enemy, and I will often release a word of what the enemy is doing or attempting to do. This is to help others, confirm what God is saying, and give direction to and encourage the people of God. But a lot of my life I have struggled with the Lord giving me a heads-up and not knowing what to do with it.

Let me give you an example. Quite a number of years ago I had a dream of a well-known general in the body of Christ, and I saw him die. I woke up, terrified. Being very new to the prophetic and not knowing what in the world had just happened, I rolled over and woke up Kevin. I told him about the dream, and I had no idea what to do about it.

I sat on the edge of my bed and I prayed for this general of the faith. Two weeks later, he was tragically killed.

This one event shook me to the core. "God, what was that? Did I not pray enough? Did I pray something wrong? Why did You share that with me?" For so long, it tormented me. So many unanswered questions, such a deep battle within me. "Should I have sent out a warning? A prayer alert?"

I sat there processing with so much going through my heart and mind. I knew that I was not responsible for what happened, but at that moment I also understood that there was a realm of hearing from God and stewarding what He releases that I had no idea about. This was a whole new area that I needed to really seek the Lord in and start to allow the Holy Spirit to teach me how to operate in it.

Recently, I had the privilege of spending some time with Patricia King, and we talked about these very topics—warnings, insights, heads-ups—and I asked her about it. She gave me a simple yet profound piece of wisdom.

She said to me often when we receive warnings we receive the revelation, but then we move out of the revelation and into our head. We move into the place of trying to work it out logically rather than running straight back to the One who gave us the revelation and asking the questions:

1. Lord, what do You want me to do with what You showed me?

2. What do I pray?

3. What is Your strategy?

I recognize this is a heavy topic, but I feel this has to be said. As believers, we need to be in a deep place of intimacy with the

Lord so that when He releases a warning we *know* how to steward the warning.

I remember another time when I was working in the marketplace, and I had a dream about one of my bosses. In the dream, I saw my boss have a heart attack and he died. I remember waking up again, so distressed. I rolled over and turned to Kevin and told him the dream. It felt like a warning dream, and there was a strong urgency to pray. So Kevin and I prayed together and cancelled any assignment of the enemy and decreed that he would live and not die. As we prayed, Kevin felt a significant shift take place that we had broken through something in the spirit.

A few weeks later, I went to work and was told that this particular boss was admitted to hospital with heart issues. I started to feel very nervous because of my dream, and I continued to pray.

I am pleased to say the story ended well. He did not die, but lived.

That dream, I believe, was a warning from the Lord to stand in prayer and to bring a change and a shift and declare the Word of God into the situation. It was to cancel any assignment and to change the situation.

So when I sat with Patricia King, her words to me were confirmation of what I have been doing for a few years now, but they were also a reminder to not allow myself to get into a place of trying to work things out when He releases things of this nature.

Often when the Lord reveals things, we may not get the understanding straight away; we get it later. I didn't know whether the dream I had about my boss was literal or not, but I went back to the Lord about it and we sought His face and prayed as we were led. Weeks later I received the revelation that that dream was a literal warning and the Lord was asking us to partner with Him to shift the circumstance and situation.

Whatever the Lord shows you—whether it's a warning, revelation, insight, or strategy—get into the habit of writing it all down. Document everything, because sometimes revelation and understanding come later down the track.

The Lord may highlight a nation, a person, a place, a city to pray into and you have no idea why. Write it down with the date and pray about it. Later on, you may receive understanding of why the Lord had you pray on that day. You never know what your prayer sowed into that person, place, or city.

Friends, do not be afraid of the Lord releasing greater insight to you as you seek His heart. The Lord's heart and will is *always* good, and He invites us into the place where we have the privilege to decree life, truth, hope, restoration, and freedom. If the Lord releases a warning or an insight, do not give in to fear. Go straight back to the source—go back to Him. Ask Him for greater revelation; ask Him for greater confirmation in the Word. Speak to those around you whom you can trust for insight, wisdom, and discernment.

He loves you so passionately. He is the perfect Father who protects you, covers you, looks out for you, shields you, upholds you, and guides you. *Always* follow your peace, and on your journey of hearing from Him never stop asking for discernment, for wisdom, and for understanding especially in stewarding warnings and greater insights of His heart.

Learning to steward greater levels of insight and warnings from His heart leads us to an even greater place of carrying His heart and partnering with Him to extend His Kingdom upon the earth.

This is the place of seeing a greater manifestation of the power of God in the lives of others and in cities and nations.

What a privilege!

PRAYER

Lord Jesus, I ask for wisdom and discernment as I continue on my journey of hearing from You. Lord, show me in greater ways how to steward Your heart with care; show me how to place value upon Your voice and what You are speaking in greater ways. Lord, train me and help me to understand and be sensitive to Your Spirit in what is to be shared and what to hold on to. I want to know Your heart, Lord; I want to know Your secrets, I want to be entrusted with greater revelations of Your heart. I'm Yours. Mold me, shape me, teach me, train me to steward the most valuable gift—the revelations of Your heart and Your voice. Thank You for the privilege that it is to be invited into that place of hearing Your voice and sharing in the whispers of Your heart in Jesus's name, amen.

DECREE

I decree the truth of Psalm 25:14 over my life: "There is a private place reserved for me, a lover of God, to sit near You and receive the revelation secrets of Your promises."

CHAPTER 5

DISTINGUISHING THE PROPHETIC VOICE OF GOD FROM THE DESTRUCTIVE VOICE OF THE ENEMY

THROUGHOUT MY JOURNEY OF HEARING THE VOICE OF GOD, one thing I have learned is that if the enemy can cause you to doubt what you hear God saying, then you can begin to lose your footing.

I know I have touched on Matthew 4:4 in earlier chapters, but I want to look at it again for a second:

> *Bread alone will not satisfy, but true life is found in every word, which constantly goes forth from God's mouth.*

So your very "true life" is found in the words constantly spoken by God. It doesn't say words that "sometimes" go forth from His mouth; it says "constantly." He's always speaking!

As the Lord is always speaking, we also have an enemy with a very clear purpose, and that is to steal, kill, and destroy, as we are shown plainly in the first part of John 10:10.

So if God is always speaking, the enemy is also always speaking, whispering, and attempting to twist what the Lord is saying. First Peter 5:8 says, *"Be well balanced and always alert, because your enemy, the devil, roams around incessantly, like a roaring lion looking for its prey to devour."*

Do you know what *incessantly* means? It means *without interruption—constantly.* The synonyms for *incessantly* are *constantly, continually, all the time, nonstop, without stopping, without a break, around the clock, interminably, unremittingly, ceaselessly, endlessly.* See the picture?

- Matthew 4:4: We live by every word that constantly goes forth from the mouth of God.

- First Peter 5:8: The enemy is roaming around incessantly—constantly looking for whom he can devour.

It is imperative that we understand that just as much as God wants to speak to us, the enemy wants to come in and twist what God is saying if he can and whisper his lies and cause doubt. "Did God really say that?" We have heard that before, haven't we?

> *Now the serpent was more crafty than any of the wild animals the Lord God had made. He said to the woman, "Did God really say, 'You must not eat from any tree in the garden'?"* (Genesis 3:1 NIV)

Part of growing in our journey with the prophetic voice of God is being able to understand the difference between His voice and the voice of the accuser. It is an ever-expanding journey for us as believers to grow in discernment and understanding of the Lord's voice until we can discern what is His voice and what isn't.

YOU WILL KNOW BY THE FRUIT

Throughout my journey I have struggled to discern God's voice from the voice of the accuser. One thing I have learned is that the *fruit* of the voice will reveal the source.

Genesis 3:1 says, *"Now the serpent was more crafty than any of the wild animals the Lord God had made"* (NIV). The word *crafty* really stood out to me in this verse, so I decided to have a look at its meaning: "clever at achieving aims by indirect or deceitful methods." Synonyms are *cunning, artful, wily, tricky, devious, deceitful, scheming, calculating.* Sounds a lot like him doesn't it? John 8:44 says:

> *He's been a murderer right from the start! He [the devil] never stood with the One who is the true Prince, for he's full of nothing but lies—lying is his native tongue. He is a master of deception and the father of lies!*

The Lord spoke to me recently concerning the way that the enemy speaks. He said that the enemy speaks using "smoke and mirrors."

Whenever the Lord speaks so specifically I, being the word nerd that I am, will dive into researching the meaning of words and terminologies, so I did just that. *Smoke and mirrors* is a phrase that means obscuring or embellishing the truth with misleading or irrelevant information.

> Something that is described as smoke and mirrors is intended to make you believe that something is being done or is true, when it is not.[1]
>
> Elaborate deception or pretense: so called after the use of smoke, mirrors, etc. by professional magicians to create an illusion.[2]

Pay particular attention to the word *pretense* in that definition: "An attempt to make something that is not the case appear true." Synonyms include *make-believe, act, sham, simulation, falsification, invention, imagination.*

The enemy's main aim is to steal, kill, and destroy and to hinder your relationship with Jesus and hearing the Lord's voice. He is crafty and a master of perversion. He roams around like a roaring lion looking for whom he may devour (see 1 Pet. 5:8).

The "fruit" of his voice is:

1. Confusion and condemnation

2. Lack of clarity

3. Lack of peace

4. Fear

The fruit of the Lord's voice is:

1. Peace

2. Empowering

3. Strengthening

4. He never contradicts His Word.

5. His voice always reveals His nature.

When the enemy speaks, I can be left feeling condemned, doubtful, and powerless; but when He speaks, I feel empowered, powerful, and always full of hope no matter what He's speaking.

Bill Johnson says, "Any area of my life in which I have no hope is under the influence of a lie." So when the father of lies speaks, there is no hope. When we align ourselves with those lies and allow them to take root, we then live under their influence and feast upon their fruit.

When growing in our understanding of the voice of God and how He speaks, we must pay particular attention to the fruit of what we are hearing and be able to recognize it for what it is. The voice of the enemy will always leave you questioning; the voice of the Lord will always leave you with peace. Sometimes when the Lord speaks it can leave our soul in a place of wrestling with what He has spoken, but in the wrestle, we find His presence, His life, His comfort, even in the places when He speaks and it challenges us or our comfort zones. The voice of God will *always* draw you closer to God and draw you to Jesus.

All of us for the rest of our lives will be growing in our understanding and discerning of the Lord's voice. May we never come to a point where we assume that we have His voice completely worked out or understood. Learning to hear His voice is an ever-growing, ever-expanding journey, and He speaks so differently and so creatively all the time.

ARE YOUR LENSES DIRTY?

When the Lord speaks, you are *invited* to see. You are invited into the place of encounter. Every word that flows from His mouth is an invitation to *see*.

There is *revelation* contained in the *invitation*. Each word that flows from His mouth is a beautifully packaged *invitation to revelation* to be released into your heart and life concerning His nature.

But notice in the garden when the serpent whispered to Eve, *"Did God really say?"* The seed of doubt and questioning was placed in Eve's heart and mind, and then she had a choice to align with the serpent or to remain true to what the Lord had said and trust in His word.

"Did God really say?" ultimately questioned and challenged the *nature* and *goodness* of God. I wonder if the battle for Eve looked a bit like this:

"If God really wants what is best for you, He wouldn't withhold this tree from you."

"If God is really good, then He would let you eat whatever you want in the garden."

"God really isn't letting you in on the full story; you're going to be left short."

"God really isn't working for you; you can't trust what He says or who He is because He is withholding this 'good thing' from you."

They are all familiar whispers aren't they? The enemy still whispers the same things today that he whispered in the garden to challenge the nature and goodness of God.

When the Lord speaks, there is an invitation into revelation and life; when the enemy speaks there's an invitation into captivity, bondage, and a place where he can torment and steal, kill, and destroy. This is why it is *so* important that as believers we know and recognize the voice, character, and nature of the Lord. We then know how to discern which voice we are hearing and aligning with. Still, things can get a little tricky and blurry when the enemy finds the *"foxes in our vineyards."*

CATCH THOSE TROUBLING FOXES

Song of Songs 2:15 says:

> *You must catch the troubling foxes, those sly little foxes that hinder our relationship. For they raid our budding vineyard of love to ruin what I've planted within you. Will you catch them and remove them for me? We will do it together.*

Brian Simmons notes in *The Sacred Journey* that the foxes mentioned here in the Song of Songs are the compromises of our hearts—the areas where we have not been fully overtaken by the revelation of His love, His goodness, His kindness. Where our immaturity and lack of revelation of who He is has kept us confined within our own fears and limited by our lack of understanding of His perfect ways.

Those "sly little foxes" will hinder our relationship with the Lord. They will raid the budding vineyard of love to ruin what God has planted within us. So the Lord puts forth an invitation to the Shulamite woman: *"Will you remove them for me? We will do it together."*

If I am not convinced of His goodness, if I am not convinced of His kindness and His love, I will find it harder to yield. I will find it harder to surrender. I will find it harder to trust, and those sly foxes will raid my vineyard of love. How we *see* Him will affect how we *hear* Him.

The "foxes" of fear, of doubt, of pain, of shame, of grief, of abandonment, of lies that we believe about ourselves or God will taint the way that I see Him. I will interpret what I hear through those lenses.

Let me give you an example.

Fear has been a huge giant that I have faced in my life. I am not talking about little fears; I am talking huge, crippling, oppressive giants of fear that numerous times would have deterred me from my calling and destiny if it wasn't for His empowerment, kindness, and continued encouragement. Time and time again I have stared giants of fear in the face and thought I was going to die and be swallowed up by the very fear that was screaming at me. Then a whisper would come—a whisper that sounded "too good to be true" that would breathe hope again into my heart.

THE ENEMY PERVERTS AND TWISTS

In my many battles with this huge giant of fear, one thing I learned was how the enemy can even take the Word of God and *twist it, pervert it* through the "foxes" and "lenses" of my distorted view of God that various experiences in my childhood and throughout my life had given me.

In one of these seasons, I was hearing the Lord saying over and over, "Behold, I am doing a new thing. Do you not perceive it? I will make rivers in the desert and streams in the wilderness" (see Isa. 43:19). It was one of my favorite verses for the longest time, until an assault of the enemy came against me. The enemy partnered intensely with a "fox" in my life—a wounding, a compromise of the heart, a painful place. He began to take the very Word of God and pervert and twist it.

"Oh, God is doing a new thing—that is going to cost you. It's going to be the new thing you are fearing. The new thing is going to be your worst nightmare in order to get you to a place of goodness or fruitfulness. God is going to make you walk through the most painful new thing He is doing. That is absolutely not your heart's desire. The change is going to be so painful, so dark, and then you will get your miracle."

Isaiah 43:19 is a verse of *hope,* it is a verse of *life*—to see God do what only God can do. It's something completely fresh, completely miraculous, a new pathway, a new level of abundant life (see John 10:10). But my heart had such deep-rooted fear, such a strong belief that God was going to make me walk my worst nightmare. The "new thing" was going to leave me in a place of such pain and heartache, and there's no way that this "new thing" could be a *good thing* for me.

Why? Because there was a deep-rooted belief system within me that God was not working for my good. That God was going to hurt me. That God was going to cause me pain. God didn't want me happy. He would always take me down the darkest, most painful, and hardest path in order to get me to my breakthrough. The path wouldn't be "blessed" because I didn't deserve to be blessed.

And one day in the midst of the wrestling, in the midst of the darkness, in the midst of the pain, it dawned on me: "I just don't believe that You are good. You are the God who takes things away."

As I found more and more of these foxes in my vineyard, they began to raid my vineyard of love. My intimacy with Him was totally hindered. I was too afraid to approach Him because He might say it's time to walk one of my greatest fears. I was too scared to approach Him because of what He might say. Everything began to crumble and shake. Instead of chasing the foxes out of my vineyard with Him, I began to agree with them. The enemy then had access to begin to come in to different areas of my life and steal, kill, and destroy.

The Lord speaks to me a lot through dreams, and I used to go to bed every night so joyful and excited about what the Lord was going to show me as I slept. Now, in this particular season, I was totally terrified to sleep because of what He might show me. Would my worst fears be played out in my night hours? Then what happened? I began to get tormented in my sleep. I had dream after dream of different expressions of fear and different scenarios playing out, and I would then spend all day in complete torment. *Is God telling me to do this?*

I remember waking up one morning after a dream that really shook me, and there really wasn't clarity if it was God or not. It could have been, but it also could not have been. But I was riddled with fear. The voices plagued me: "God is giving you a heads-up of what He is about to make you do." My heart was full of fear; I was living in a state of panic, no peace, certainly no hope, but all of this had an "element of truth" to it.

Like the Shulamite woman, we *are* called out of our comfort zones. We are called to come higher. We are called to a place of leaving behind old mindsets and ways of slavery and moving into greater freedom and intimacy with Him. Jesus doesn't exist for our comfort and to come and take up residence in our comfort zones, and because of so much fear in my life I could feel my heart screaming, "Please don't do this to me. Come and meet me in my place of comfort!"

But see, I kept getting tripped up on God's "*way.*" The "*way*" He was going to set me free was going to be my worst nightmare. My heart would scream, *"Of course You are going to set me free in this hellish way!"* Those foxes had really taken root.

So there was an element of truth in it all—I was being challenged to live a life of deeper trust, deeper surrender, and deeper yieldedness to Him. But the enemy used that truth in my heart and whispered, "See, you're not surrendered. If He says *go* and *do* you are refusing to because of fear, so God is going to make you face your fear. Your days ahead look pretty dark and have a huge cost. There's a cost to following Jesus—this is yours, and of course He would ask this of you."

The battle intensified so much, I ran to Him, screaming my heart out, "*God, I will go and I will do whatever You want me to do but I hate this. I don't want to but I will!*"

My soul was in absolute torment.

Then a whisper came and life returned to my heart. I still remember the day—in the midst of the deepest pain and the darkest moment of so much fear—when He spoke to me: "I am not tearing your dream away from you. That dream you carry in your heart—that's from Me. I just want to set you free *in your dream*, give you back your dream and with *increase*. I want you free to *enjoy* your dream, and with this incredible deep fear you are not living in the joy and freedom I want you to in your dream and destiny. Lana, *this isn't a subtraction. It's a multiplication.*"

I remember the moment. It was as if I had been drowning in the seas, battered in the storm, unable to stand anymore. The despair, hopelessness, and pain were so unbearable, and that whisper was like someone put oxygen back into my heart and lungs. I literally *gasped* and took a deep breath, and I heard a whisper come from my heart that I had not heard before: "*Hang on, are You really that good? Are You really that kind?*"

As the journey progressed, the battle continued to rage, the enemy continued to scream, the fear continued to raise up its ugly head—but you know what happened? I began to move to a deeper level of discerning the fruit of His voice—the hope, the peace, the love, the kindness, the encouragement, the overwhelming sense of *life*. Even if I was being asked to step out of my comfort zone, there was peace, hope, and life.

DESPAIR, HOPELESSNESS, PAIN, AND TORMENT—THAT'S NOT GOD!

I began to notice that every time the enemy would speak or twist Scripture, attempting to sound like God, I would be left with despair, hopelessness, incredible pain, and torment.

It began to become clear to me. This battle wasn't so much about me stepping out and facing fear—although that's important. But this battle was about catching the "foxes" in the vineyard of my heart and soul—the compromises that had sprung forth and taken root because of wounding and lies and unbelief. Those "foxes" were being *healed* and *removed* by me trusting His voice, trusting those whispers of love and hope, and allowing Him to do the work in me that was needed. To root out the weeds in the garden of my heart.

The whole battle wasn't about Him taking something away; it was about Him leading me through a journey to recapture my heart and reveal His goodness and kindness to me. His love, His voice, His spoken word by the power of the Holy Spirit would then empower me to stand in the storm. To command fear to be silent. To come to the place of believing that with Him, I can do anything. His voice of love, of hope, of encouragement, of peace, of "come up higher" was cleaning the lenses of my heart from the stains and the dirt that life had thrown at me and tainted my view of Him.

Minute by minute, inch by inch, every little whisper that brought me peace and life in the midst of the storm took the revelation a little deeper in my heart that He was good. That He wasn't ripping me off; I wasn't going to be left short. I was actually being increased and expanded to live the dream and destiny He had given me with freedom.

HIS VOICE EMPOWERS, GIVES LIFE, AND CALLS YOU HIGHER

That's His voice! The voice that empowers! The voice that calls you higher. There's always turbulence in "going up" and "coming up higher." Our foxes are exposed in the shaking and the rattling. When you have nothing else to hold on to but His voice to remove the despair, the hopelessness, and the fear, a resolve begins to be birthed in you that says, "No matter what the reality in the natural looks like, my *true* reality is *every word* that comes out of the mouth of God. I live by *that* and not by my screaming emotions, my circumstances, my false securities, or things going right in my life. I live securely and firmly in the revelation of His nature through His Word and His whispers in my life."

What He speaks transcends my reality. His voice imparts to me, shifts things for me, breaks things off me, heals me, delivers me, matures me, and strengthens me.

When I am resolved in Him, I can do and face anything. I know His nature, His goodness, His love, the fruit of His voice; I know He never changes and there's no darkness with Him. That's the type of maturity and resolve that He wants to build in His people. Maturity doesn't hide behind walls of fear like the Shulamite woman did when He called her to go higher. Maturity hears His voice, knows His love, and can follow wherever He leads.

You can "go and do" for the Lord, you can minister, you can obey and still have areas of the heart that are closed off to Him, foxes raiding your vineyard, and a hindered level of intimacy.

He cares so much about your heart. He cares so much about you having a deep intimacy with Him. When you are confident in hearing His voice and you understand the way He speaks and who He is, you awaken as the courageous warrior and overcomer you are.

You and I will stand in any circumstance in life with confidence, peace, security, and even joy when we understand the way He speaks. The fruit of His voice and the revelation of His nature through what He declares through His Word and other ways that He speaks, will see us through every storm.

He isn't looking for slaves who just go and obey to keep Him happy. He's looking for lovers, an overcoming Bride. Those who have found Him in the fire, found Him in the dark, found Him in the struggle and allowed Him into the deepest crevices of their hearts. We will remove the foxes together and live a life of surrender and yieldedness feasting upon every word flowing from His mouth. It's a beautiful place.

> *There's a private place reserved for the lovers of God,*
> *where they sit near him and receive the revelation-*
> *secrets of his promises* (Psalm 25:14).

In our pursuit of His voice, it is imperative that we continue to invite Him daily into our hearts and souls to release the revelation of who He is. I'm going to take you further into this subject as we dive into the next chapter! See you there!

▌Prayer

Lord, I thank You that Your voice empowers, Your voice imparts, Your voice shifts, Your voice transcends my earthly reality. Lord, help me to discern the "fruit" of what I am hearing. As I go deeper into the Word, teach me how to recognize Your voice more clearly and not be ignorant of the enemy's schemes. I invite You, Holy Spirit, to come and reveal any "foxes" that I have allowed into my vineyard and strengthen me to remove these foxes from our vineyard of intimacy.

▌Decree

I decree in Jesus's name that Your voice brings life, it calls me higher; Your voice calls me into greater revelation of who You are and who I am in You. I decree in Jesus's name that Your voice is powerful, Lord, and I am empowered by what You speak and by the power of Your Spirit. I am not ignorant of the enemy's schemes and lies, but I am a lover and carrier of the truth of Your Word that sets me free and empowers me in greater ways to live a life of discerning Your voice from the voice of the enemy, in Jesus's name.

NOTES

1. *Cambridge Advanced Learner's Dictionary and Thesaurus,* s.v. "Smoke and mirrors," accessed February 20, 2018, https://dictionary.cambridge.org/us/dictionary/english/smoke-and-mirrors.

2. *Webster's New World College Dictionary, 4th Edition,* s.v. "Smoke and mirrors," accessed February 20, 2018, https://www.collinsdictionary.com/dictionary/english/smoke-and-mirrors.

CHAPTER 6

WHAT WE BELIEVE ABOUT GOD DETERMINES HOW WE HEAR HIS VOICE

WHAT WE BELIEVE ABOUT HIM AFFECTS EVERYTHING. IF MY revelation of Him is that He is not good or that He is not the perfect example of love, I am hindered in my approach to Him and my understanding and interpretation when He speaks. The lenses of our hearts need to be continually cleansed by the Holy Spirit and the revelation of Jesus—the God-Man, the perfect representation of the Father (see John 14:9). It is imperative to be continually growing in the revelation of His nature.

It is vital that I understand His heart and know that when I approach Him I will be celebrated and not condemned. I need to know that He doesn't point out all my flaws, but He calls me higher by calling out how He sees me and my destiny.

Even in the place of conviction, it's imperative that we see His heart—a good Father who is bringing us to the greater place of walking in the manifestation of the abundant life.

HE CHANGES HOW YOU SEE

In the midst of one of those seasons when the Lord was really challenging my "lenses," He began to show me just how much my level of revelation of His goodness and kindness affected how I approached Him and how I heard His voice. It affected my level of faith. It determined whether I drew close or pulled away—even what I expected Him to say.

I remember this one occasion when the Lord really taught me, again, that valuable lesson that one word from Him, one vision, one revelation changes everything. I am to live off revelation and not what's going on around me. On this particular day, I was being bombarded with lies of the enemy. There was such a battle of the mind against my identity. Such accusation coming against me about who I was or mistakes I had made in the past.

I was sitting with the Lord and giving Him permission to come in and deal with the root of these lies and mindsets. They were tormenting me, and the enemy was using them as a landing pad to really steal my peace. "Lord, please set me free. Help me. Save me. Free me," flowed from my heart and out of my mouth. Suddenly, I had this vision, so clearly, right before my eyes.

I saw Jesus, my beautiful Jesus, and He was kneeling against what looked like a tree stump—battered, broken, bruised, beaten, bloody. I saw the enemy on one side accusing me, and on the other side I saw a man with a whip. The enemy would look at me and throw his accusation at me. Then Jesus, my beautiful Jesus, would receive a lashing of the whip across His back. He would cry out and then decree the truth about who I was.

For *every* accusation of the enemy against me, Jesus took it upon Himself and decreed truth over me—the truth of who I was in Him. I watched as this went on, over and over and over again. His blood, His precious blood was being shed for me as He declared truth over me.

Followed closely by that vision, I had another vision where He showed me accusations and lies that others and the enemy had spoken over my life. These were the lies I had believed—line after line after line of lies about who I was and His goodness.

I saw His blood spill over those pages. All those lies I believed about Him and His nature, all the lies I believed about me and who I am were covered, completely covered in His blood. In the middle of the pages a beautiful rose appeared, and He whispered to me, "You are the rose of My heart. I am rewriting the story!"

Over the next few months, His voice rebuilt my heart. Over the next few months, His truth rebuilt my story. His goodness and love healed the broken places and began to show me more of His unconditional love and His kindness toward me. This brought me to a whole new level of His delight in me, not because of what I do but because I am His.

His voice exposed the foxes in my life, and we removed them together. His voice exposes the lies of the enemy. His voice empowers and invites us to come up higher. His voice heals, awakens, restores, refreshes, and redeems.

Rooted in Love

"As your roots go down deep into My love, then your decree will be Ephesians 3:20." For years I have been decreeing and prophesying the beautiful promise of Ephesians 3:20:

> *Never doubt God's mighty power to work in you and accomplish all this. He will achieve infinitely more than your greatest request, your most unbelievable dream, and exceed your wildest imagination! He will outdo them all, for his miraculous power constantly energizes you.*

I love that verse! Don't you?

I remember a beautiful vision I had where the Lord took me into a "blueprints and planning room" in heaven and He was unravelling scrolls. The plans that He had for His people were written on these scrolls. I looked at these scrolls and noticed at the bottom were the "greatest dreams and desires" of His people. I remember wondering why they were at the bottom, and the Lord knew my thoughts. He looked at me and smiled and said, "Your greatest request, that's where I begin." I was blown away!

The point wasn't that He would fulfill everything I asked for. I have certainly asked for things in my life that, if He had of given them to me at the time, it wouldn't have worked out well. He knows perfectly what to give me and especially *when*. The point was that His plans are so much bigger than I can imagine. What I can "dream up" is often so small compared to what He has planned. He wanted to show me just what a wonderful, big, amazing God He is and His extravagant goodness in the plans He has for our lives (see Jer. 29:11).

At times, as I have slept in the night, I have heard the Lord speaking in my dreams over and over all night long saying, "I really am the God of Ephesians 3:20. I really am the God of Ephesians 3:20."

He really is the God of Ephesians 3:20!

So for years I have been decreeing that verse over my own life and prophesying it for myself and others, and then the Lord said to me one day out of the blue, "Look at the verses before that, Lana."

So off I go, back to verses 17-19:

> *Then, by constantly using your faith, the life of Christ will be released deep inside you, and the resting place of his love will become the very source and root of your life Then you will be empowered to discover what every holy one experiences—the great magnitude of the astonishing love of Christ in all its dimensions. How deeply intimate and far-reaching is his love! How enduring and inclusive it is! Endless love beyond measurement that transcends our understanding—this extravagant love pours into you until you are filled to overflowing with the fullness of God!*

Then it goes on to verse 20 that we looked at: *"Never doubt God's mighty power."* So by constantly using your faith, the life of Christ will be released deep inside you.

So we use our faith, we believe what He says, we trust in His Word, we align with His truth, we renew our mind—then we see His life released deeper inside us. And the resting place of His love will become the very source and root of our life, providing us with a secure foundation that grows and grows.

LOVE CHANGES EVERYTHING

Anything else that is our source or root is removed as we come into a deeper place of rest in His love. Our foundation becomes more and more secure. We grow in Jesus as our source, our life, our root system. We see our strength increased in our life in Him, and we are empowered to see what? *His love!*

We move deeper into a place of the revelation of His love. We see His unconditional love for us, not based upon works but based upon *whose* we are. Out of the place where I am "in over my head" in the most glorious way, seeing His love in a way that I cannot even comprehend because it is so huge and magnificent, I am undone by this revelation that He loves me. Out of that place, the decree of *faith* bubbles up inside me: *"Now to Him who is able to do...."*

"Never doubt God's mighty power at work in you to accomplish all of this."

In seeing His love, my lenses get cleaned. My faith increases. The foxes are removed from my life as I partner with Him. Everything changes in the revelation of His love. In the revelation of seeing that He *is* love and He *is perfect love*, I then *believe* that He accomplishes by His mighty power greater things than I could *ever* imagine *in* my life and *through* my life. I move from the place of being bound in lies of who He is and my identity in Him, to *awake* in His love, and I decree with faith and belief:

> *"What no eye has seen, what no ear has heard, and what no human mind has conceived"*—the things God has prepared for those who love him (1 Corinthians 2:9 NIV).

I move into a greater place of freedom to dream big, to enlarge my faith, to raise my hopes.

His voice and the revelation of His love removes the limitations. His voice and revelation of His love heals my heart and rebuilds truth within me and breaks the chains of the enemy around my heart and mind. Those two encounters did that very thing for me, and led me to a deeper place of decreeing:

> I **do not doubt** God's mighty power to work in me and accomplish all this. He will achieve infinitely more than my greatest request, my most unbelievable dream, and exceed my wildest imagination. He will outdo them all, for His miraculous power constantly energizes me.

FREE, UNLIMITED ACCESS!

After those two profound encounters, there was something the Lord taught me. The vision, the prophetic word, the encounter with Him—when you receive it, you then have free unlimited access into that place. It's like a portal for you, a well of revelation, a well of intimacy between you and the Lord alone, and it doesn't just stop the first time you have the encounter.

Let me explain to you what I mean.

In 2015, I was sitting with the Lord in my lounge room, worship music filling the room as I cried out to see Him and hear His voice—not for any other reason but to be with Him. To know Him more, to feel His touch, to look Him in the eyes, to know Him in a way I've never known Him before. Suddenly, I had the strongest sense that He was about to show me something profound.

For the next 30 minutes, I had one of the most vivid encounters with the Lord that I have ever had. This was one of those encounters where the Lord took me into the heavenly realms and showed me things I could never have imagined. It was similar to my first encounter with the Lord, when He took me into the throne room and showed me all the jewels on the walls. In this moment, in my lounge room in 2015, it happened again.

I am going to share this encounter with you next, but I am going to share it in a third-person narrative—a story. In this encounter, I am Purity. It is my story. I had this radical, life-changing encounter with the Lord, and when I came out of it the Lord told me two things.

1. "This encounter is a place of *access* for you. You can come to Me at any time and ask Me to take you back into that place. You can ask Me to show you more. You can ask Me to reveal more to you."

See, once the encounter had taken place, once the word was given to me, once the vision happened, I had complete permission to ask the Lord to reveal more and to *meditate, revisit,* and live that encounter. What do I mean? I cannot tell you how many times I have had an encounter with the Lord, I have had a word from God, I have heard His voice, and then daily I have meditated upon what He has spoken and asked for more. I have been intentional to live and immerse myself in that revelation and encounter. I simply close my eyes, put on worship, and ask Him to reveal more, take me back. Then He takes me back into that vision, that encounter, that place of revelation, and He opens up more than I received the first time.

Often we can be too quick to rush along and long for the next encounter and revelation. We must always be hungry for more. Like Kathryn Kuhlman said, "There's always more," and there *is* always more, but those encounters with the Lord are your "wells" that you have dug in your relationship with Him.

It's not that we live on yesterday's manna—not at all. We are to seek fresh manna daily, but I want you to see that in encountering God, hearing His voice, and seeing His heart, you can *revisit* those revelations and encounters *as well as* seeking for more. Ask Him lots and lots of question; be like a child, hungry to see and hear more. The danger is seeing those beautiful encounters we have had in the past as "one off" things. "Oh, that was an amazing encounter I had with Jesus. That was an amazing vision. That word I received was amazing; what He said blew my socks off. Wow." And then we move on.

What if there are more layers the Lord wants to show you and reveal to you as you *revisit* with holy inquisitiveness to see, hear, and know more?

2.   The revelation that I received in this encounter was for me personally, but it was also for many others.

The Lord told me to rewrite the encounter as a parable and release it publicly. This was *such* a difficult thing for me to do because this was a profound encounter and so close to my heart. But the Lord was *very* clear that the revelation I received and the impartation that was in this encounter would set many others free, heal them, encourage them, deliver them, but most importantly open up a portal for them to encounter the Lord in a deeper way in the heavenly realms like I did.

So I obeyed and I released it. To this day, two years later, I still see this word being reposted, shared, and people being touched and ministered to because of His presence and breath upon this word.

In your encounters with Him—your visions, what you hear, your journey of hearing His voice—the revelation that you receive from the Lord is a priceless, beautiful treasure for you. But these revelations, when shared by the leading of the Spirit, can minister, refresh, encourage, and build up others.

So let me introduce you to Purity.

This is Purity's story. I want you to meet Purity. Purity is a lover of Jesus. Purity is one who continues to seek hard after His heart. Purity is one who stands on the front line and is partnering with Him in what He is doing on the earth. Purity has suffered much, endured much, and walked deep valleys with Him while the storms raged; she is one who has danced and cried with joy on the mountaintops.

Purity is one who knows the secret place well and her greatest desire is to know Him. Purity in this season has felt the sudden onslaught of the fiery darts and is weary from the battle. She began to feel the "tug" to withdraw and find the cave to hide in away from the eyeballing stare of the enemy.

Purity misplaced boldness and forgot the authority that was hers because of the weariness that had become so heavy from the battle. The wounds from the darts throbbed with an ache Purity had not known before.

In Purity's place of despair, the place of almost giving up, Purity began to feel His wooing of love: "Come away with Me—I want to show you something."

Purity had hardly any strength to press forward any more or go deeper. The best Purity could do was stay collapsed at the feet of the One who held her heart in His hands. Suddenly, He, beautiful Jesus, reached down and lifted her high off the ground through a portal, and she entered into a whole new dimension.

Purity found herself standing before a *mansion,* and she knew she was in heaven. She looked to her left, and she saw Jesus standing beside her. She was standing there with Him, in *awe* of this *mansion.*

It had all the colors of the rainbow all over it, sparkling with swirls like glitter. It was like the house was alive and breathing. This house was *full* of life. Jesus grabbed her hand, and He smiled at her and said: "I have brought you here to show you a representation of the impact you are having on earth in Me. Do not ever doubt the impact you are having and the treasures in heaven that are being stored up for you. This is just the beginning of what is stored up for you. Come, let Me show you something."

He then walked with Purity hand in hand up to this mansion, and He opened the white picket fence. As they stepped onto the footpath, they heard this roar of applause. All around the house, around the picket fence were all these people who were shining brighter than anything Purity had ever seen.

They were the great cloud of witnesses, and they were applauding loudly.

Purity walked hand in hand with Jesus into this mansion, yet she couldn't see much inside except polished floorboards. She instantly had the sense that she couldn't see any more in this house because her mission on this earth still had a long way to go and was nowhere near finished yet, but a stirring began to fill her heart that it was going to get a lot *fuller* from this point on.

Purity felt His strong yet gentle hand motion her to the right, and Jesus spoke: "After the many assaults that you have faced, this has now been opened up to you."

And there was a *huge* door before her that was covered in jewels.

He opened it, and inside there was a river flowing, but this river had *huge* waves and it was flowing all through the room. It was so beautiful; she was completely immersed in these waves.

The Lord led Purity into the middle of this room filled with the rainbow waves, and He began to laugh and laugh and laugh—such joy. Purity began to cry and cry and cry as the grief and pain in her heart began to pour out. She knew instantly that He was restoring her heart.

As the grief and pain came out, it was swallowed up by these beautiful rainbow waves, and in the place where this pain and grief was, her heart was being filled with this rainbow-colored water.

Instantly she knew that *He was changing the atmosphere in* her promises, *in* her destiny. He was turning the pain and the grief into *joy*. His laugh had two different sounds. It was a laugh of pure joy, but also a laugh at the enemy.

As he laughed at the enemy, it carried *such* authority. As each laugh left His mouth, it was as if His laughs were messages, carrying sentences of authority toward the enemy.

The first time He laughed at the enemy, the words boomed: "You think you hit Purity hard; your attempts are petty. You just wait and see what I am going to do to you through her. I am *laughing* at your attempts. You just watch and see what I am about to do in and through her. Thank you for positioning Purity for greater promotion."

Once the pain had left her heart, she began to laugh and laugh with Him, their heads flung back in laughter. He then looked into the middle of this room of rainbow waves and reached in deeper than Purity could see, and He pulled out four flags. He said to her, "These are to take back with you."

The first flag was purple and written on it in *huge* letters were the words *favor and promotion*. The Lord then began to explain to her that new doors and floors of favor and promotion were opening up to her.

The second flag was orange and it said *honor*. The Lord went on to say that there was going to be greater visible manifestations of His honor and vindication over her life. This would bring great change and transition in the body of Christ as she ministered to restore honor in the Bride.

The third flag was green and it said *finances*. The Lord spoke: "Where the enemy has stolen and broken in the area of finances I am going to bring huge breakthrough and provision leading to *huge* testimony." The Lord was breaking a lot of financial burdens the enemy had brought upon her.

The fourth flag was blue, yet in the light it was all the colors of the rainbow and it said *double portion of revelation and accuracy*. The Lord explained that Purity was being positioned for greater clarity the moment the enemy decided to go "head to head" with her.

The Lord then turned to Purity and with a smile on His face He said, "Purity, it's time to go." They walked back out of this room, out of the house, down the front steps of the porch, down the path, and the crowd was still outside clapping and cheering and saying, "You are doing *so* well; it *only gets better from here.*"

They were *so* excited and shouted, "You just *wait and see* what happens from here. *Yay! Yay! Yay!*"

As the Lord led Purity back to the portal to leave this heavenly encounter, a handful of angelic hosts crossed her path.

They spoke to her with tear-filled eyes and said, "It is *such an honor* to be assigned to you and work with you in partnership with Him." They handed Purity a little wooden box, and as she opened the box there were two keys.

The first key said *access to angelic encounters*. The Lord was moving Purity into a season of greater encounters with the angelic hosts of heaven.

The second key said *access to this place*. An invitation was being released to Purity to come back in and out of this mansion when she needed to.

The angelic hosts spoke: "This is *your* special place."

Purity then moved through the portal and exited the heavenly encounter, but Purity was healed, restored, refreshed, and positioned for greater breakthrough than she had ever known. All the darts the enemy had thrown at her to stop her from moving forward actually positioned her for greater promotion in Him. Not only was there restoration, but she had moved into a realm that was completely *new*.

ACTIVATION

There is more for you. So much more. I encourage you to go back to times you have heard from the Lord, revisit them, and ask for more. If you don't have that special place, that special encounter with Him, ask Him to show you the special place He has for you. There is so much more He wants to reveal to you.

Lord, release an impartation right now for deeper encounter. Lord, I ask that You would release a deeper hunger to revisit the places where You have spoken and revealed Your heart and goodness. Lord, take them deeper than they have ever seen. May they go to a whole new level of revelation, awakening, insight, and encounter with You. Release the fire of Your love to burn within them like never before. Cleanse their lenses with Your love, Lord, to see You as You really are in deeper ways. Take them deeper into heavenly realities and realms of Your Spirit in Jesus's name, amen.

PRAYER

Holy Spirit, I invite You to come right now and reveal to me any lies that I have believed about the goodness and nature of God. I ask Holy Spirit right now that You would reveal any places in my heart where I have believed anything about Your nature, God, that doesn't line up with the truth of who You are.

Take a moment right now and as the Holy Spirit brings up any wrong beliefs about His goodness, kindness, and love, repent of those lies and ask the Holy Spirit to reveal the truth of who He is, His goodness, and His love.

He is a good Father—He is always good! He loves you with an unconditional love. He delights in you because you are His.

Every gift God freely gives us is good and perfect, streaming down from the Father of lights, who shines from the heavens with no hidden shadow or darkness and is never subject to change (James 1:17).

Lord, I ask that You would take me into a deeper season of knowing Your love. Take my roots down deeper into the revelation of Your love. Let the fire of Your love fall and burn away anything that has hindered what I have believed about You and how I see You. I decree that Your love changes everything, so I invite You right now, Holy Spirit, to come with a fresh baptism of the fire of Your love. Consume me afresh in Jesus's name, amen.

DECREE

There is so much more for me! I decree there are deeper encounters with the Lord awaiting me right now. I decree there is so much more He wants to reveal to me. I decree there are deeper revelations and treasures that are going to be given to me as I revisit encounters I have had with the Lord. I decree as I dive deeper into those special places with Him I will never be the same, in Jesus's name.

CHAPTER 7

THE DIVINE
INTERRUPTION OF
THE VOICE OF GOD

IN CHAPTER 2, I BRIEFLY LOOKED AT FIRST SAMUEL 3:4-10 when I felt like Samuel—*hearing* but not knowing it was God. Let's recap:

> *Then the Lord called Samuel. Samuel answered,*
> *"Here I am." And he ran to Eli and said, "Here I*
> *am; you called me." But Eli said, "I did not call;*
> *go back and lie down." So he went and lay down.*
> *Again the Lord called, "Samuel!" And Samuel*
> *got up and went to Eli and said, "Here I am; you*
> *called me." "My son," Eli said, "I did not call; go*
> *back and lie down." Now Samuel did not yet know*
> *the Lord: The word of the Lord had not yet been*

revealed to him. A third time the Lord called, "Samuel!" And Samuel got up and went to Eli and said, "Here I am; you called me." Then Eli realized that the Lord was calling the boy. So Eli told Samuel, "Go and lie down, and if he calls you, say, 'Speak, Lord, for your servant is listening.'" So Samuel went and lay down in his place. The Lord came and stood there, calling as at the other times, "Samuel! Samuel!" Then Samuel said, "Speak, for your servant is listening."

I want to look at this passage, but from a different perspective. I want to look at it from the perspective of the *divine interruption of His voice.* When He speaks and when He interrupts, it changes everything. Even though we may be experiencing things that are negative, walking through situations that are unfavorable, or believing deception, one word from the Lord is a divine interruption that breaks the attack and cycle of the enemy in our lives.

This has happened to me time and time again in my life. As I have battled the giant of fear for most of my life, I notice that when I hear one word from His heart the chains of fear and dread break in an instant. I can be standing in the place of such turmoil, such hardship, such pain, and such torment from the enemy and the opposition coming against me, but suddenly one word from the Lord interrupts that attack and peace is restored into my situation. Some of the most powerful breakthroughs and deliverances of God that I have had in my life have come in moments when He has *spoken* and the cycle, the attack, the opposition of the enemy has *broken.*

Let me give you an example. As I talked about in Chapter 4, whenever I would come up against any type of battle with the enemy he would always use fear to attempt to cripple me, hinder me, and cause me to pull back. So, a lot of my life I have faced incredibly irrational fears as the enemy has whispered lies into my heart or thoughts have gone through my head that have crippled my heart with fear in an instant.

Well, the day I am going to tell you about was one of those days. We were on holiday as a family and decided to go for a drive. I was really struggling on this day, because for the week before that, everywhere I had been looking I had been seeing news reports or hearing stories of car accidents.

This horrible fear would come and whisper to me, "That's going to happen to you and your family." Now, that's pretty clearly not God, right? But when you have a "landing place" of fear in your heart, a whisper like that comes to you and it "hooks in." So I began to do the only thing I knew to do. Kevin and I prayed together, and then I started decreeing the opposite, quoting the Word of God, praying protection over us all, cancelling assignments of the enemy, and asking others to pray.

I was a ball of fear. My anxiety levels were high, and this accusation was whispering to me and lingering all around, and I had no breakthrough. I couldn't seem to push through this murky, hazy, lingering feeling of fear, foreboding, and dread. Kevin and I prayed together before we left, I decreed Psalm 91, and off we went.

We went for this beautiful drive—perfect scenery, the wind in my hair, the sun shining, my boys giggling away in the background—yet I could not be present in the moment because I was *so* afraid of our "drive." I was decreeing under my breath, praising the Lord and thanking Him for His protection, but my heart was so afraid. Then, suddenly, I heard the words so quietly, yet with so much power: "Lana, you are safe! Lana, you are all safe! I am protecting you! No harm will come to you."

Within an *instant,* and I kid you not, the anxiety drained out of my heart, and I literally felt like I could breathe. I took a deep breath and felt like my peace was restored to me. The divine interruption of His voice *broke* the cycle of torment of the enemy that kept me in a place of such fear. The words were full of life, love, hope, peace, heaven's reality; they invaded my heart, invaded the atmosphere of fear around me, and *shifted it.*

HIS VOICE TRANSFORMS

The whispers of His heart are love bombs; when they are released into our lives, they change everything. They *transform.* I say it all the time, and I will say it for the rest of my life. It is not just a "nice thing to say" that His voice changes everything, His voice really does change everything. One word from His heart released into our lives can heal our hearts, break the chains, bring freedom, shift the atmosphere, and bring life.

Transform means to make a thorough or dramatic change in form, appearance, or character. His voice brings thorough or dramatic change; that is why it is *so* important that we know and recognize the voice of God and then *engage* in what He is speaking to shift the atmosphere. We will look at *engaging* with what He speaks in the next chapter, but my heart right now is that you *see* how the *divine interruption* of the voice of God changes everything.

But as His voice can interrupt and change everything, the enemy is always looking to interrupt with his lies and his whispers.

FALSITIES

The enemy attempts to interrupt with *falsities.* What is a *falsity?* A fact that is untrue, incorrect, or insincere. Synonyms include *untruthfulness, untruth, fallaciousness, falseness, falsehood, fictitiousness, inaccuracy, mendacity, fabrication, dishonest,* and *deceit.* The enemy sends these *falsities* to interrupt our lives to keep us bound—to keep us in a place where our vision and our sensitivity to the Lord's voice is hindered.

The enemy knows the power of God's voice—the power of the Lord speaking into your life. When the Lord speaks, His voice creates and establishes. The Lord is *so* committed to His Word being performed in your life that He watches over it (see Jer. 1:12). Remember how we talked earlier about paying attention to repetition. The Lord loves you so much and is so committed to you hearing from Him, that out of His love He repeats His word over and over and over again until you get it. The Lord speaks *so* much every day, but we can miss it because we aren't looking or paying attention. But He is committed to watching over His Word to perform it, and He will continue to interrupt our lives with His language—we just need to be "tuned in" to recognize it. That's why it's so important to cultivate a lifestyle of leaning in, looking for Him everywhere, and asking for greater wisdom and discernment to recognize His voice.

The Lord repeats, and so does the enemy. The enemy repeats over and over and over again, because he's looking for *agreement*— our *engaging* with him and his lies.

FALSE TIES

When the Lord showed me how the enemy sends *falsities* to interrupt our lives and bring us to a place of bondage through our agreement, I had a vision. I clearly saw the word *falsities* and it turned to *false ties.*

The enemy attempts to tamper with the "airwaves" in the spirit; he twists and attempts to cause a static, a haze, a blinding, a blocking of ears. To disrupt and interrupt what God is saying and doing, he causes fear and twisting in dreams, major confusion, and hindrance of sight. But recently, I heard the Lord say: "Where the enemy has attempted to *interrupt*, I come with the divine *interrupt* to *shake up.*"

And that is *exactly* what happened to me in the car that day. The enemy came to *interrupt* with his falsities and his lies, but then the Lord came with His *divine interruption* to *shake up!*

When the Lord *interrupts* our day-to-day lives with His voice, it is always a reminder to us that there is *so much more* awaiting us in our relationship with Him. Every day of our lives as His people, there is a greater awakening that takes place to hearing His voice.

HE INTERRUPTS IN DREAMS

I love the way that the Lord *interrupts* in dreams. You and I can be battling with *falsities* of the enemy attempting to create *false ties* in our lives—we can be pressing through all day, fighting back with the Word—and then when we go to bed at night, the Lord ministers to us as we sleep.

I am a huge dreamer. So many healings and deliverances I have received in my life have been through dreams. Rather than devoting one whole chapter to dreams, I felt the Lord wanted me to intermittently share keys I have received in my dreams throughout various chapters. One of my most profound divine interruptions that came through a dream happened in 2017, when I walked out this very chapter I am writing about.

I was seeking the Lord one afternoon, just delighting in His presence and loving on Him, and I heard these words: "Lana, you are about to enter the dark night of the soul; but do not worry, I will be with you."

You may not believe what I did next. I rebuked that voice! I thought, "That cannot be God," and I started to list all the reasons in my mind why in the world it would not be the season for a dark night of the soul.

It came again: "Lana, you are about to enter the dark night of the soul; but do not worry, I will be with you!"

Again, I fought with it. "This cannot be God!" I was petrified of what that "dark night of the soul" meant, but it didn't sound good to me. Because of fear in my heart, I focused upon the "dark night of the soul" rather than the promise "but do not worry, I will be with you."

Two weeks after I heard about that dark night of the soul, I entered a dark night of the soul. A *falsity* came to me, attempting to "sound like God," and whispered a lie to me. It wasn't God, and that was clear to everyone around me because the fruit of what I heard wasn't peace, joy, hope, and life but fear, dread, anxiety, and complete lack of peace for both Kevin and I.

The *very night* of the day this falsity hit me, I went to sleep and the divine interruption of His voice came to me. I had a dream where the Lord showed me the enemy coming against me, trying to kill me to *stop* what God was doing in my life. At the end of the dream, I *removed* the foothold that this falsity had found in my heart. Somewhere the enemy had found a fear in my heart and had hooked this falsity into my heart so the torment had a place to land.

Night and day this falsity would come against me with the thought, "What if this is God? What if...what *if...what if...?*" More fear, more anxiety, more torment—but the divine interruption of the voice of the Lord through that dream became an *anchor point* for me in the battle of the dark night that I was walking through. I would keep coming back to that dream; it was a center point for me where the Lord *interrupted* the cycle. The enemy was trying to lure me into a place of false ties to his lies and bondage, which would have significantly hindered me from moving into all God had for me.

Many months went by. Every day I was on my face, crying out to the Lord to hear His voice; His voice literally became my every breath. Worship, praise, and the secret place were the very air that I breathed. It was my oxygen. It was the place where I would snuggle into Him and cry out to hear Him, and as He spoke, as I worshiped, all torment and fear would leave. I was able to breathe peace, my vision clear, my discernment back: *"That's right, this voice isn't God!"* Then I would come out of my secret place, and this *falsity* would hit me again.

One night, I went to bed after months upon months of fighting this thing. It was the greatest torment I had ever faced, and I thought I was not going to make it. Then, the Lord interrupted my darkness again with His beautiful voice.

I woke up in the middle of the night and couldn't get back to sleep. My eyes were drawn to the open door of our bedroom, and as I lay there the Lord's voice came to me *so loudly* it startled me— but in such a glorious way! "Lana, the angel of blessing has arrived at your door. The angel of blessing will yield its sword, activating the threshold to release the season of the rain of greater blessing upon you and your family. You will have double what the locust stole and ate. This is My promise to you! There is going to be such blessing upon you and your family. The angel of blessing has a double-edged sword to redeem and restore."

His voice interrupted the battle I was in so significantly; a tremendous shift happened that night. My peace was restored to a level I hadn't had in that season. My confidence, faith, and joy began to be restored, and the strength and faith in what He was saying rapidly increased. The divine interruption of His voice was heralding, "The light is at the end of the tunnel."

As I sought the Lord the next few days and spoke to some people close to me about this encounter, I knew that this was the same type of angel that was sent before Isaac's servant to "prosper his way" in Genesis 24.

A *key* that the Lord showed me was to look at which *interruption* I choose to *feast upon.*

1. Do I choose to feast on the *interruption* of the enemy?

2. Do I choose to feast on the *interruption* of God?

WHATEVER I FEAST ON, I EMPOWER

Because whichever one *I feast on, I empower!*

The very next morning, I took the divine interruption of that encounter where He spoke and I knew there was an angel standing at our bedroom door, and I began to *feast* upon the promises that He had given me. Part of my feasting upon that divine interruption was I asked the Lord for *more.*

Whenever the Lord speaks, I *always* ask for more. I want to feast, eat, and suck (in a gloriously good hungry way) *every morsel* of revelation and goodness *He* wants to give me. I don't want to just take a bite and walk away; *I want it all*. So, I asked Him for more. "Lord, would You give me a dream and show me this angel of blessing?"

That night I went to bed after asking to see the angel of blessing and the Lord interrupted my sleep again. I had another dream, and guess what He showed me? He showed me the angel of blessing that had been assigned to me and my family. The Lord showed me the series of events that had taken place in my life and what had happened in the spirit. At the end of this horrible onslaught in the spirit I had faced, in the dream the angel of blessing walked up to me and opened up a precious box—the type of box in which you keep something *very* precious, valuable, and expensive. When the angel opened it, inside was the *double-edged sword* that the Lord has spoken about.

The angel looked at me in the dream and told me that they were now being sent by the Lord with this double-edged sword into the enemy's camp to bring back the spoils to me. The Lord was redeeming and restoring in my life all that the enemy had stolen.

I woke up! What a divine interruption of my sleep! What a glorious, precious treasure from the Lord.

I want you to hear this. This isn't just "for Lana"—this is for all believers. This is for the children of God. He wants to interrupt our lives every day with His voice more and more. He wants to show us His face more and more every day, but I pose a question to you that He has asked me so much over my life.

Do you give Him permission to interrupt your life *however* He chooses to interrupt? Do you have eyes to see and ears to hear to recognize when He does show up and divinely interrupts?

In the *divine interruption* of God in our lives, we need:

1. The hunger in the positioning. "Interrupt my life, Lord, with Your voice in whatever way You choose."

2. "Give me the eyes to see and ears to hear Your divine interruption when it comes."

OUT-OF-THE-BOX DIVINE INTERRUPTIONS

The divine interruption of God can come clearly, like the dream I had or the voice I heard in the car whispering His encouragement and His protection of me and my family. But sometimes, the divine interruption of God comes in ways that we may not understand.

For example, one of the messages I have carried this year has been the message of victory. That this is the season of the birthing of the overcomers. This is the season when God is awakening His people in greater ways to the victory that is already ours in Christ. The awakening that we are fighting *from* victory, not *for* it.

> *Yet even in the midst of all these things, we triumph over them all, for God has made us to be more than conquerors, and his demonstrated love is our glorious victory over everything!* (Romans 8:37)

He is encouraging us more and more to step into our authority in Him, taking the victory of Christ, and making it our own—walking it out. Rising up with the cry that says "No more devil! That's my land! That belongs to me," and evicting him with the Word of God.

Well, do you know how the Lord interrupted my life with this message? Through a dream.

Jesus came to me in a dream at the end of 2016, and He said to me, "Lana, there are new shoes for the new season."

And do you know what Jesus handed me in the dream? A pair of Nike runners. Now, in the dream I was wondering why I needed Nike runners. Was the Lord suggesting I needed to exercise more in this season?

I had *no* idea what He was saying. All I knew was that the Lord had interrupted my life again with His beautiful voice, but this time it came in a way that I didn't understand or expect. I woke up and could not shake the feeling that I needed to go and buy a pair of Nike runners, still thinking, *"I need to exercise more."* So off I went to find the exact pair of runners from my dream.

Who would have thought you could get Nike runners in *every color* of the rainbow? But mine *had* to be black and white because that's what the Lord had given me in the dream. I was trying not to tell the sales assistant, "Listen! Jesus came to me in a dream and handed me *black and white* Nike runners—they *need* to be black and white!" You can imagine how that would have gone down.

Well, there were none in the store my size, and as I was about to leave, he said to me, "Hang on! I think I have one pair left in the back; let me check." He ran back and brought a shoe box out and opened it up—guess what? There were my Nikes from my dream.

With everything in me fighting to not cry—because I was in a divine moment when something the Lord showed me in a dream was before me in the natural—I mumbled the words, "Let me try them on." I tried them on, and I am sure you can guess the end of the story. Perfect fit!

And just because the Lord is *so* fun, the style of Nikes I got had a little inscription on the side that said "Nike Zoom." Just like the

Lord! I had been prophesying acceleration everywhere I was going, and here it was on the side of my shoes. So there's *no* doubt that it was God, right?

I went back to my hotel, and I pressed in to the Lord for the revelation of this divine interruption dream. I was crying out, worshiping, in the Word, waiting for an angel to show up, a vision—anything! But there was nothing.

I was pressing in hard when He whispered, "Lana, what have I taught you to do when I highlight a symbol?"

Aha! I research!

So I started researching the word *Nike* and guess what? The word *Nike* comes from the Greek word *nikos*, meaning "victory" in Scripture. And in the natural, the Nike slogan is "Just do it."

The Lord's voice divinely interrupted my dreams, spoke in a totally *unexpected* way, and birthed a message in me for *my own* life and for the body of Christ—awakening the overcomers. The year of the victory of God being manifested in the natural in a greater way. Taking the victory of Christ and running with it. Taking back the ground the enemy stole. Facing *fear* and *just doing it!*

So much came from that divine interruption of His voice in my dream, but what would have happened if I didn't continue to *pause* and *press in* for the *understanding* and the *revelation* of that divine interruption? I would have missed out on that glorious word the Lord wanted to share with me. That word *broke* things off my life, and everywhere I have gone and released that word I have seen the *divine interruption* of His voice, released through the prophetic word, break off *so much* in the lives of others.

The divine interruption of His voice will heal you, it will deliver you, it will bring you higher into heaven's reality, it will draw you closer to His heart than you have ever been. It will shift your perspective; it will break the *false ties* the enemy is attempting to lure you into. It will shift your mindset, it will breathe new life into your heart, it will awaken you to the overcomer you are. It will refresh you, rejuvenate you, awaken you, and train you in greater ways to be sensitive to His voice.

But you know what is so beautiful about the divine interruptions of God? *You will be left in awe and wonder!*

God wants to lead you and me into a deeper place of the *awe* and *wonder* of who He is and His goodness, His power, His love, and His kindness. The divine interruptions of His voice will leave you undone by His beauty, the revelation of the God who is *present*—He cares, He loves. The divine interruptions of God leave you in awe with your jaw on the floor—*He* just showed up!

What joy! What life! What deep awakening takes place in the divine interruptions of His voice! Don't you want His voice to interrupt your days? I do! Every day, my heart explodes and burns with a hunger and fire that cries out, "*Lord, invade my world! Lord, interrupt my life with Your voice!*"

Some of my greatest moments of joy have been in those moments when His voice has interrupted my day. All of a sudden, I feel more alive, more awakened and connected to my beautiful King than I did five minutes before. The same is true for you!

RECOGNITION AND SENSITIVITY

One word from His mouth, changes everything.

Are you crying out for more of those divine interruptions of God in your life? Are you asking God for the eyes to see and ears to hear to recognize them?

Because there are some amazing, sovereign, divine interruptions of God upon you that are going to be so glorious. They will shift a season in your life and bring a significant breakthrough. They'll open up a whole new realm of understanding the language of the Spirit and ways that He speaks. The sovereign, divine interruptions of God and His voice will transform you, change your life, change your path. Some could be a Damascus road experience; others will take you from the edge of the waters of the Spirit, just dangling your toes in the realm of the supernatural, to in over your head experiencing God and hearing His voice in a way that is so completely beautiful and overwhelming in such a joy-filled and life-giving way.

I want you to be awake to it more than ever. I want you to ask the Holy Spirit for more of those divine interruptions of His voice if you want them.

I believe that the body of Christ is moving further and further into that place of the great awakening, where every believer is confident in hearing the voice of their Shepherd. They will know how to hear, prophesy, and live by the words that He speaks. They will no longer rely on the prophets to receive the revelation and live from word to word. They will live deep in the secret place of intimacy with Him, feasting at the banqueting table of revelation that He is offering them one on one; then the prophetic word will confirm and guide.

The Lord's heart is for us all to hear from Him. No one but me is responsible for my secret place with the Lord. No one but you is responsible for your secret place. We must cultivate the garden of our intimacy and secret place with Him and live off the revelation He is giving us, not the revelation the prophets are releasing as our source. That is living so far below what the Lord has for you. The beautiful call of God in the divine interruption of His voice beckons us to *awaken* and come up higher than we ever have in *recognition* and *sensitivity* to His voice.

Do not be tied to the things that are *false*. Do not be tied to the things that raise themselves up against the knowledge of who He is (see 2 Cor. 10:5). Take the *divine interruptions* of His voice and feast upon them. Eat every part, meditate upon them, decree them, pray them through, and ask for more. Demolish the arguments—feast, feast, feast, and don't stop feasting upon truth. The Lord is setting a table before you in the presence of your enemies.

Choosing to align with fear, death, and lies, putting trust in those things, trusting in the "pharaoh" or the "ways of Egypt" will lead to slavery again. God wants to lead us out into victory, and the new thing He is doing requires that decision from us as God's people to *continue to choose life* through our *surrender, trust, decree, yieldedness,* and *humility.*

Don't trust in what you have always known in your "slave mentality." Invite Him in through your intimacy with Him, your total surrender, praying in the Spirit, and renewing your mind with the Word to *prepare you* for the *new* that is *upon you.* I believe there's an impartation available right now, even as you read these words, to receive and recognize the divine interruptions of His voice in *more ways* than you have ever experienced before—if you want to receive it.

A great awakening of the *divine interruption* of the *voice of God* is upon you! I prophesy over you right now in the name of

Jesus Christ that a whole new level of *awe* and *wonder* of who God is and His goodness and kindness will be revealed to you through His *divine* interruptions in your life, in Jesus's name.

Jump all in to this deeper level available before you! It's going to change your life!

PRAYER

*Lord, I am all in! I want to see You, I want to know You, I want to encounter You, and I want all that You have for me, and I know there is more. Holy Spirit, awaken me in greater ways to the divine interruptions of God. Teach me to **stop** and lean into You when You interrupt. Teach me to respond; teach me to navigate the divine interruptions. Help me to take moments to stop and ponder Your interruptions. Lord, I lay down my life again to You. I surrender again; I cry out again, "Have Your way, Lord." I give You permission to come and interrupt my life with Your goodness, Your love, Your ways, and Your kindness in Jesus's name, amen.*

DECREE

I decree in Jesus's name that I will be attentive to the divine interruptions of His voice in more ways than I have experienced before. I decree that I will not live in the **falsities** that the enemy attempts to bring upon me; I will not partner with them, in Jesus's name, and I decree that this is a new day of freedom for me in recognizing the divine interruptions of God and being **tied** to the Word of God and His truths in deeper ways, in Jesus's name. I decree that any boxes I have tried to place the Lord in are broken right now in Jesus's name, and I invite You, Lord, to come and show Yourself to me in new and fresh ways, increasing my sensitivity to Your divine interruptions and teaching me to respond, in Jesus's name.

CHAPTER 8

ENGAGE WITH HEAVEN: HOW TO RESPOND TO GOD'S PROPHETIC VOICE

ONE THING THAT I HAVE ENDEAVORED TO DO THROUGHOUT my journey of knowing Jesus and learning to hear His voice is to always place value upon and steward what He is speaking to me. I never want to come to a place where I have become so complacent or familiar with God speaking to me that I casually hear what He is saying and walk away. My heart has always been to *stop* and put *value* upon what He is speaking.

I have seen time and time again that when I have stopped and placed value upon what He is saying, He always adds more. There is always increase. He is looking for people who will *stop* and *steward* what He is speaking and releasing. Stewarding what God is speaking and releasing fine-tunes our ability to hear His voice.

There have been so many times in my life when the Lord has shown me something about someone and I have stepped out on what I have heard and released a word of encouragement. Sometimes I'm shaking in my boots because I wasn't given the "full picture," but in that place the Lord has been training me and fine-tuning my hearing. Seeing Him show up and come through gives me confidence and greater understanding for the next time I step out.

In previous chapters I have shared with you a little of my journey of how I do that. I am looking for Him, so I pay attention to repetition and I research symbols that He highlights. The heart of the Lord when He speaks to us is that He wants us to *engage* with Him and He wants us to engage with what He is speaking and releasing. That is part of our relationship with Him and part of the stewardship of hearing His voice.

For a long time in my life, I would receive prophetic words from God and I would just "shelve them" and hope that one day they would miraculously come to pass. I didn't understand that every time the Lord spoke it was an invitation into engaging with Him and engaging with His Word and His heart.

Engage means to participate or be involved in, to occupy or attract. I feel the heart of God so strongly as I write this. I feel His whisper so beautifully, so tenderly, dripping with intimacy, dripping with invitation: "Every word that I speak is an *invitation* to *engage* with My people, to *engage* you with Me. The invitation to *engage* is *meant* to lead to *engagement*." When we hear His voice we must steward what we are hearing by being intentional in our *engagement* with what He is releasing.

LINGER

"God shouts His truths and whispers His secrets."
—BOBBY CONNER

Over my life I have sought His heart on how to live a life that is not only *engaged* with what He is speaking but also with carrying His heart and knowing Him. I never want to operate in a gifting and not know His heart. We know that the gifts and callings are irrevocable (see Rom. 11:29), so it is possible to move in a gift of prophecy and not know Him or His heart (see Matt. 7:23). What a scary place!

As I sought out greater ways to stay *engaged* and live a life of *engagement*, I had a profound dream in January 2017 that gave me greater verbiage for what I had been carrying for many years. In this dream, I heard the Lord saying over and over, "Where are those who will linger? Where are those who will linger in this season of acceleration?" As I was waking, He began speaking to me that those who linger will be those He will entrust with the secrets of His heart.

The word *linger* means to stay in a place longer than necessary because of a reluctance to leave. I was left undone! I heard the heart of God filled with such deep longing for His people, yearning to know them and for them to enjoy His presence. To simply be with Him, to sit as two best friends sit together, even without words— just enjoying each other.

It was the place of invitation from the Lord into deeper stewardship of His presence and His heart. It's that deep place that says, "Lord, I love You, I value You, and I value who You are and what You speak, so I will not rush to run out of Your presence. I will linger because I have one heart agenda, and that is to *know You* and *be with You.*"

For just one day of intimacy with you is like a thousand days of joy rolled into one! I'd rather stand at the threshold in front of the Gate Beautiful, ready to go in and worship my God, than to live my life without you in the most beautiful palace of the wicked (Psalm 84:10).

The Lord then highlighted Joshua to me:

Whenever Moses entered the tent, the pillar of cloud would descend and stand at the entrance of the tent; and the Lord would speak with Moses. When all the people saw the pillar of cloud standing at the entrance of the tent, all the people would arise and worship, each at the entrance of his tent. Thus the Lord used to speak to Moses face to face, just as a man speaks to his friend. When Moses returned to the camp, his servant Joshua, the son of Nun, a young man, would not depart from the tent (Exodus 33:9-11 NASB).

Joshua *lingered!*

We can look throughout Scripture at other biblical characters and see the same heart within them to linger.

Moses *lingered!* David *lingered!*

There is a private place reserved for the lovers of God, where they sit near him and receive the revelation-secrets of his promises (Psalm 25:14).

Over the last few years I have had numerous visions, encounters with God's heart, and dreams around the very same theme. God is looking for those who will linger. Those who will *look* and *engage* not only with what He is saying but *who He is.* He is looking for those who will take the time to *engage* with Him—not to get something from Him, not to have the latest prophetic word, not to take what He is saying and carry it, but not have His heart. Whether He is speaking to us for ourselves or someone else, we must live in a place where we linger, not only to carry His words but to carry His heart.

His eyes are roaming! His eyes are searching! He's looking! Does that not cause you to be undone? The heart of Almighty God is looking for those who will *linger.* Why? So He can *reveal* His heart and fellowship with His people and His love, goodness, and kindness can be revealed to us and through us.

There is *no end* to discovering the heart of God, and He's inviting you and me in. Let us not take His invitation lightly! Let us not cast away His question. Let us cry out together, asking that His Spirit burn that invitation *so deep* within us that we are *moved!* We are shaken out of any areas of complacency and awakened to deeper intimacy and friendship with our Beloved. Let us be *intentional* to *invite* His Spirit to convict us to continue to *engage* with His heart when we hear His voice. To carry His heart and His secrets, a crucial key is to be people who learn to and continue to *linger* in His presence.

No one else is responsible for my secret place with Jesus. No one is else is responsible for how much oil I have in my lamp. I do not want to be one who is found not ready, needing to borrow oil from another like we are shown in the parable of the ten virgins in Matthew 25.

I had a dream recently. The Lord showed me that for those who linger in His presence He would release greater strategy and blueprints to for their lives, communities, cities, and nations. He would disciple them in the perspective of heaven. He showed me that those who intentionally marinate will accelerate; they will hold keys of insight, strategy, and revelation.

He is looking for those who will linger. Not in order to *get* but to *be* with Him. The fruit of your lingering will be greater than you can imagine. The creativity and strategy of heaven you will carry from the place of your lingering will bring shift and change wherever He shows you to apply it.

I can still hear His whisper: "Where are those who will linger?"

ACTIVATE YOUR FAITH AND ALIGN YOUR DECREE

> *That's what the Scripture means when it says: "I have made you the father of many nations." He is our example and father, for in God's presence he believed that God can raise the dead and call into being things that don't even exist yet. Against all odds, when it looked hopeless, Abraham believed the promise and expected God to fulfill it. He took God at his word, and as a result he became the father of many nations. God's declaration over him came to pass: "Your descendants will be so many that they will be impossible to count!"* (Romans 4:17-18)

Abraham engaged with the Word of God to him through his trust and his faith. Abraham had to *engage* to take responsibility to activate that word in his life through his faith. He trusted in what God said and His faithful nature to fulfill that which He spoke.

When God speaks, He is looking for the activation of our faith and our alignment with His voice. Sometimes when the Lord speaks, His Word is like a seed released into our hearts and lives. We cultivate the environment in which that seed will grow. We must cultivate our hearts and lives to *make room* and the *right environment* for those seeds to grow, and the seeds grow in the place of faith and trust in God.

Part of the task of cultivating the right environment to steward His promise is done in *process*. I have often said that the two things I never wanted to mention in my prayers as a young believer were patience and process, because both in my mind equaled *pain*. Just the thought of those two words made me cringe. I thought the more I prayed about patience or process, the more I would end up facing situations where I would need more patience and process. That equaled, "It's going to be a long and painful process to get to see your promise fulfilled."

THAT "P" WORD—PROCESS!

I read different stories in Scripture about how the Lord released promises to His people, and often there was an intense process to steward that word and birth that promise. It scared me. I had a major fear of pain, and I didn't even realize it. I would read the story of Joseph and see the amazing dreams, the promises from God, and I would cringe all the way through the story until he got to the palace and then I was fine. I hoped the less I asked God to teach me about process the less I would find myself needing to go through a horrible process to get to my promises. How naïve and silly I was!

So can you guess what happened? Can you guess what the Lord started to do? He started to heal me and show me the power of process. Some of my processes I thought I was going to die in, yet I would come out the other side. Time and time again I would see the power of process and the beautiful things that the Lord does *in* process—that place between the promise and its fulfillment.

I began to learn that God cares about the destination, but He really cares about the "in between" place—the process place. He is the God of process. Now I realize—many, many years later—that what we need to move into our promise, what we need to carry the promise is given to us and happens in the process. There is so much glorious preparation that His Spirit accomplishes in the process.

One of the greatest things that I have learned—through *many* situations where I thought I was going to die with my promise—is the power of activating my faith with what He is saying and aligning my decree with His decree. It continues to be revealed within me that our *true reality* is the *unseen realm*. Our true reality is what *He says*. In the in-between place, the place of waiting for our promises to be fulfilled, we are shown again and again and again that our *true reality* is living by every word that comes out of His mouth and speaking things that are not as they are (see Matt. 4:4; Rom. 4:17).

In First Kings 18, Elijah heard the sound of rain:

> *Then Elijah said to Ahab, "Go get something to eat and drink, for I hear a mighty rainstorm coming!"* (1 Kings 18:41 NLT)

You know what I love about the passage? Elijah *heard* the sound of a mighty rainstorm coming before it manifested. Elijah's reality was not what was going on around him—there wasn't any sign of the rain cloud about to manifest—but his reality was "God said rain is coming."

> *So King Ahab went to eat and drink. At the same time Elijah climbed to the top of Mount Carmel,*

> *where he bent down to the ground with his head*
> *between his knees* (1 Kings 18:42 NCV).

The place of intercession. The place of focus. The place where his ears were covered by his knees. The place of intentionality to focus only upon what God had said, engaging in the true reality—the unseen realm, the realm of what God had decreed. Such beautiful alignment and positioning to speak forth those things that are not as they though they are.

I love that the prophetic word of God establishes, transforms, creates, and manifests the unseen realm into the seen realm. The decree of our mouths aligning with the decree of heaven establishes His agenda upon the earth.

WINGED WARRIORS

In 2016, I had a dream where I heard the Lord decreeing all night, "I am now raising up My winged warriors."

As I woke from my sleep, I asked the Lord, "Lord, did You say winged warriors? What in the world is a winged warrior?"

Do you want to know what He replied to me? "Lana, it's a warrior with wings!"

I was no more enlightened! But as always, I knew that the Lord was inviting me into a deeper dialogue. That's one of the things I absolutely love about the Lord. His voice draws us, His voice beckons us, His voice invites us into a deeper place of intimacy and communion.

So I laid my lack of understanding on the table (not like He didn't already know). "Okay, Lord, but I still don't understand— what is a warrior with wings?" Then, I clearly heard Him say, "Ephesians 2:6."

He raised us up with Christ the exalted One, and we ascended with him into the glorious perfection and authority of the heavenly realm, for we are now co-seated as one with Christ! (Ephesians 2:6)

Suddenly, the understanding came to me. The Lord was calling His people higher; He was calling His people to live from "our seated place," where we are totally awake to the authority that we have in Christ. We "war" from our seat, from that heavenly place. Part of that "warring from my seat" involves taking the Scriptures, the *logos* (inspired written Word) and the *rhema* word of God (the spoken word) and aligning and declaring it. It was all about perspective. The Lord was challenging me personally on perspective—how do I live my life? Do I war from the "ground," affected by my circumstances, or am I awake to the power that I am seated in heavenly places? I have the privilege of partnering with the *logos* and *rhema* word of God to decree what He is decreeing to see the reality of heaven begin to manifest and change circumstances and situations upon the earth. This is the place where we are awakened as His people to the reality that we are already overcomers.

Yet even in the midst of all these things, we triumph over them all, for God has made us to be more than conquerors, and his demonstrated love is our glorious victory over everything (Romans 8:37).

So reading that, I see that in the midst of anything I face I triumph over it all. Why? Not because of my own strength, my own ability, or anything that I can do; it is because *He* has made me a conqueror through His demonstrated love. His death and resurrection has given me the victory, and it is a victory that always remains. I have already won. I am not fighting *for* victory, I am fighting *from* it. The victory of Christ is eternal. He has won! I have already won! My seated position is the *winning* position in Him. So I live in the One who *is* victory; I live in the One who is the great Victor. What He speaks carries the impartation of breakthrough—it carries the impartation of victory because it flows from the One who *is* victory.

THE WORD OF GOD IS POWERFUL

> *For as the rain and the snow come down from heaven, and do not return there without watering the earth and making it bear and sprout, and furnishing the seed to the sower and bread to the eater; so will My word be which goes forth from My mouth; it will not return to Me empty, without accomplishing what I desire, and without succeeding in the matter for which I sent it* (Isaiah 55:10-11 NASB).

> *For we have the living Word of God, which is full of energy, and it pierces more sharply than a two-edged sword. It will even penetrate to the very core of our being where soul and spirit, bone and marrow meet! It interprets and reveals the true thoughts and secret motives of our hearts* (Hebrews 4:12).

The Word of God is powerful. The words that flow from His mouth are alive. He carries the words of eternal life (see Matt. 4:4; John 6:68), and you and I have the glorious privilege to sow into our lives and the lives of others, cities, and nations through our declarations that echo His heart.

I remind myself often of what the Lord is speaking over my life. What am I reading in Scripture? What is the Lord breathing on? I take those declarations and decree them over my life and the lives of others. I realize that the greatest prophet over my life is me. I have the power in my tongue to speak life or death, blessing or cursing over my life and the lives of others (see Prov. 18:21; James 3:5-6).

For my own life, I want to be one who is always speaking what He is speaking. I want to live so deeply in intimate relationship with Him that He shares the very secrets of His heart, and I can stand in the confidence of knowing Him. I want to know His nature and decree what He is speaking even if it's unpopular, even if it's not what others are saying. I have spent my life sowing into my relationship with Him to know His heart and be one voice in the beautiful body of Christ who releases the words of life that flow from His heart.

Will I be the voice of life when others are speaking death? Will I be the voice of hope when circumstances are saying there's no reason to hope? Will I be the one who speaks heaven's agenda into the earth and the lives of others no matter what I see in the natural? I have given my life for this; I have given everything to be one He would entrust His heart and His words to, no matter the cost. His heart so beautiful, so loving, so good, so kind, so just, so perfect and full of mercy, and you and I have the privilege of carrying that heart. I never want to come to a place in my life where I don't live in the awe of that privilege.

YOU HAVE A VOICE!

To be a mouthpiece on the earth is one of the greatest treasures He has given me. But you know what I love? We are *all* His mouthpieces! Each one of us. You are His mouthpiece. I am His mouthpiece. We just have different roles and expressions of that mouthpiece.

As a wife, you are a mouthpiece to your husband. As a mother, you are a mouthpiece to your children. As a teacher, you are a mouthpiece to your students. As a brother or sister, you are a mouthpiece to your siblings. As a son or a daughter, you are a mouthpiece to your parents. *Wherever* you go, you are a mouthpiece. You may be called as a prophet. You may be called as an apostle. You may be called as a pastor, a leader—whatever the role, you are a mouthpiece.

But you know what it boils down to?

YOUR POSITION NEVER CHANGES

When roles change, there is *one position* that *never* changes. You are a child of God. You are a son or daughter of the King of kings and Lord of lords. Your glorious Father absolutely adores you! He lavishes you with so much adoration. He loves you not because of what you do but because of who you are. He rejoices and delights over you with singing—not because of how many things you have done right today or how much time you have spent with Him; He delights over you today because you are His. His love for you *never* changes. Your *position* never changes. You won't wake up tomorrow morning and not be His child. You are always His child. You are always His beloved. He formed you in your mother's womb and He knows you (see Jer. 1:5; Ps. 139:13).

So your *position* never changes. That's who you are, and as a child of God you are called to be *salt* and *light* to the world. You are called to take the Gospel to all the earth, to release the Kingdom, to shift atmospheres, to release life. There are *many ways* you can do that as a child of God, but one of the most beautiful ways to do that is to be a voice of *hope* and *encouragement*.

Today, I challenge you—will you see the spheres of influence He has given you and see that you are a *mouthpiece* for the King of kings and the Lord of lords? That is not something to fear—that is something to rejoice in. Do not be afraid of speaking. Choose to be encouraging. Choose to speak life. It doesn't mean you have to walk up to someone and say, "Thus saith the Lord," and have an angel show up (although angels showing up is always fun). Be a conduit of His presence and *life*. Be encouraging and *always* speak life. Be one who is committed to *speak life* and *encouragement everywhere* you go.

So why am I saying all of this? Because I want you to see today that you are powerful! You are a mouthpiece *already!* God has *already* entrusted you to speak life and hope and encouragement. Do you realize that *one decree* over someone's life that is the echo of what God is decreeing can *change everything?*

What I *love* to do in my *intentional engaging* with God is to ask the Lord what He is decreeing over my children or husband or city or nation. When He speaks it, then I *repeat it.* We are going to look at this in more detail in another chapter, but I love what Job 22:27-29 says:

> *You will pray to Him, and He will hear you, and you will pay your vows. You will also decide and decree a thing, and it will be established for you; and the light [of God's favor] will shine upon your ways. When you are cast down and humbled, you will speak with confidence, and the humble person He will lift up and save* (AMP).

What a promise! You will pray to Him and He will hear you! You will decide and decree a thing and it will be established for you.

There is so much power in decree, and God backs up His Word. He really does! When we decree what is on His heart, He backs it up. He confirms His Word. I have seen so much fear over the years. *"What if I decree something and it isn't God?"* I always say—stay *founded* and *grounded* in the Word. God isn't going to give you something to decree that is outside of His Word. The Lord does not contradict His Word, so when I hear God tell me to decree something or I see something in the spirit in a vision, I always ask for scriptural backup. If the Lord is saying, "Decree an increase of favor," I will search the Scriptures and ask the Lord for a verse on favor. If I have a vision where I see the Lord releasing healing, I will find a verse on healing and decree it. If the Lord is telling me to decree the assignments of the enemy become null and void, I will grab a Scripture and decree no weapon formed against me or my family shall prosper.

FIND YOUR VOICE IN SCRIPTURE, STOP, THEN MEDITATE ON IT

God may highlight a "theme" to me of what He wants me to decree, and if He doesn't give me a Scripture, it's my responsibility to go and search the Word for it. Then I'll stop there, meditate upon it, and decree it. Bill Johnson calls it finding your "voice" in Scripture. He specifically mentioned doing this in the book of Psalms, which is what I have done for many, many years.

We must be founded and grounded in the Word; we must *know* the Word and decree it. When we hear something that we think may be God asking us to decree, we know that if it's not from God it will contradict the Word and go against His nature.

Chasing after revelations or experiences and moving away from the Word of God is a very dangerous place. That is why when I teach on hearing from God, I spend a lot of time encouraging people to *be in* the Word and *know* the Word. Spend time knowing His nature and character and verses of Scripture so you can *test* what you hear.

It is not God's heart that we decree *death* or *curses* over people, cities, or nations. We are to decree *life*. Even when God may show something negative that may be going on in a situation, that doesn't mean God wants us to repeat it. We must *push past* the negative and ask God for the *answer*. What is the *life answer*? Find the *life answer* in His heart and in the Word and *decree life, decree hope, decree Jesus* as the *answer* and leave the rest to Him.

As the people of God with the power of life and death in our tongues and the ability to shift atmospheres, to prophesy over our own lives and the lives of others, we cannot be people who walk around prophesying death or curses. We are conduits of life, hope, and love.

WHAT IS ON YOUR LIPS?

I had a very powerful dream in the middle of 2017 where I saw a lady approach me who had cancer. She began to tell me how many of God's people were suffering with this horrible disease. I agreed, and my heart was breaking for how the enemy was stealing, killing, and destroying through this insidious disease. All of a sudden I felt a wave of faith rise up in me so powerfully in this dream. I looked at her and I said, "Yes, cancer seems to be on many lips right now." I then saw a tidal wave of healing come crashing into the body of Christ, and I looked at her and I said, "*Wow!* Just imagine how God's people's faith is going to radically increase as they see this mighty healing wave that is crashing in and increasing in the body of Christ to heal cancer and remove its power on a level we have never seen!" I then woke up.

The Lord spoke to me a lot through that dream. The most obvious was the healing wave of His Spirit that is going to continue to increase in the church and then out into the world to see cancer's power removed. There will be many more signs and wonders of healing and creative miracles in the area where this horrible disease has taken so many lives. I also felt the Lord say that it would lose its power in the lives of believers so dramatically that it would no longer be the word on everyone's lips.

The third thing the Lord spoke to me was that "cancer on everyone's lips" was also a reminder to the body of Christ to not have *death* on our lips. To not carry death words everywhere. To not be sowing death with words. To not be sowing curses with words, but to be people who speak and decree *life*.

Friends, today I want to encourage you—you have the power to shift atmospheres, decree life, decree encouragement, hope, healing, and freedom wherever you go. Feast upon His Word, study it, meditate on it, engage in it, linger with Him. Ask Him what He is dreaming about, what He is decreeing, what He is seeing, and *repeat it*.

Remember, *every time* you decree, *every time* you intercede, *every time* you *repeat* what He is saying, you are *filling* the bowls of heaven; you are *sowing* in the Spirit into what He is doing—into breakthrough, shift, and release of His presence and Kingdom. You are partnering with what He is doing to bring His reality to earth.

Write out the decrees He is giving you and keep *repeating* what He is saying. Watch the glorious things He will do. *Today* could be the day that one decree sees the bowls of heaven *tip,* and that one decree *changes everything!*

PRAYER

*Lord Jesus, I choose again today to engage in what You are speaking over my life. I choose again today to engage in Your Word, Your promises over my life, the prophetic words I have been given. I choose again today to remain intentionally engaged. Lord, I pray that You would continue to strengthen me in my process. I choose again today to speak life, to speak hope, to speak encouragement over my life and the lives of others. I pray that You would continue to teach me to meditate on Your Word and linger with You and decree what You are saying. Continue to teach me, Lord, to live "from my seat" in heavenly places with You. Train me in Your perspective and awaken me to the truth that I fight not **for** victory but from it. Thank You for **Your victory,** Your death and resurrection; the same power that raised Christ from the dead lives in me. Thank You, Jesus, that I am an overcomer, that I have triumphed in You. Continue to awaken me to heavenly realities to live a life of engagement in Jesus's name, amen.*

DECREE

I am an overcomer in Jesus's name. I am seated in heavenly places with Christ Jesus. I engage with the Word of God and His promises over my life.

I am a mouthpiece who decrees blessing and life and not death. I decree that in my process, right now, that God's promises over my life are true, no matter what my eyes see. I decree that I trust in God and what He has spoken to me, and I will remain **engaged** in His Word and what He has spoken to me in Jesus's name.

CHAPTER 9

RELEASING
THE VOICE

*There is not in the world a kind of life more
sweet and delightful, than that of a continual
conversation with God; those only can
comprehend it who practise and experience it.*

—BROTHER LAWRENCE,
The Practice of the Presence of God

I LOVE THIS BROTHER LAWRENCE QUOTE—IT'S SO RICH, IT'S
so beautiful, it's so weighty. This is the place of continual conversation with God and living in the practice and experience of it. The
heart of God is that we live in that very place of continual conversation every day, but it doesn't and isn't meant to stay within the
four walls of our house or secret place.

What do I mean by that? One of the most powerful things that we can recognize is this: "You are powerful everywhere you go." I talked a little bit about this in Chapter 8—that the Lord has given you a sphere of influence. No matter what you do for a job, whatever your position and journey is in life right now, the truth remains the same. *You are powerful because Christ lives in you.*

> *I have been crucified with Christ and I no longer live, but Christ lives in me. The life I now live in the body, I live by faith in the Son of God, who loved me and gave himself for me* (Galatians 2:20 NIV).

So you are powerful *everywhere* you go. Everywhere you go, you carry His presence. Everywhere you go, you are carrying the light and love of Jesus. Everywhere you go, you shift atmospheres. You can walk into a room and pray and declare and shift what is going on in that room because you have walked in with Him.

A friend of mine, Doug Firebaugh, says, "There has never been another *you*. There will never be another *now*. Do something *legendary!*"

I say something similar to that *so* often. There isn't another *you,* and what God has given *you* is unique; it's beautiful. The way that you hear from God is unique. How you shine Jesus and release Him to this world through your gifts and talents is unique and needed. No one else can release in this world what you carry. There is *not* another you! *You* are powerful and what *you carry* is powerful!

SHINE! SHINE! SHINE!

You can walk into your favorite store, I can walk into my favorite coffee shop, and have an opportunity right then and there to release the love of Jesus, to extend the Kingdom, to speak life.

I want to say this at the outset too. We all have different personalities—some are extroverts, some are introverts. Some find it natural to walk up to someone and talk to them outside the four walls of the church; others don't, and that's okay. We are all different. My heart is to encourage us all, as God's people with different personalities, to not allow our personalities to become an excuse for not stepping out or seeking the Lord for ways to shine. We must be pressing in and asking the Lord for creative ways to release His Kingdom, to be a light, to be a voice, to shine. We aren't called to stay in our comfort zones; we are called to step out in faith and shine for Him and preach the Gospel. Let's not let fear stop us but continue to ask the Holy Spirit to lead us according to our personality to release our unique expression of His love and light upon this earth.

I have talked quite a lot about the privilege it is to hear from God, but it is also an incredible privilege to be *used by God* to bring the Lord's words of encouragement, life, and comfort wherever we go.

I believe the Lord's heart is for the people of God to be fully awake and fully present wherever they go, "in tune" and looking for Him. Throughout this book I have talked a lot about looking for God everywhere, and we really must be people who are looking for Him everywhere. I love Matthew 5:13-16:

> *Your lives are like salt among the people. But if you, like salt, become bland, how can your "saltiness" be restored? Flavorless salt is good for nothing and will be thrown out and trampled on by others. Your lives light up the world. Let others see your light from a distance, for how can you hide a city that stands on a hilltop? ...Instead, it's placed where*

everyone in the house can benefit from its light. So don't hide your light! Let it shine brightly before others, so that the commendable things you do will shine as light upon them, and then they will give their praise to your Father in heaven.

You carry His presence and you carry His light and you are not meant to be hidden. Everywhere you go, you are meant to shine! Shine! Shine! Shine! Shine the love of Jesus! Shine the light of Jesus! Shine the hope of Jesus! Shine the truth of Jesus! Shine the goodness and kindness of Jesus!

I remember a while ago having some time with the Lord and the Lord met me in a powerful way. I was so overwhelmed by His presence. You know those times when He shows up so strongly. When He feels closer than ever, and His voice is clearer than ever. That moment when nothing else matters but the encounter that you are having with Him.

Well, I was having one of those times with the Lord. I remember weeping with joy and love for Him filling my heart, and I mumbled the words, "Lord, I never want this to end. I never want this to end. I feel like I am going to explode. I have so much fire, joy, passion, and love for You within me."

And do you know what the Lord said to me? The first thing He said to me was, "Lana, it only gets better from here!"

I was having a life-changing moment with the Lord, one of the greatest encounters, and He whispered it only gets better from here. My heart came alive! My heart burned! Those seven words reverberated through my entire being, shouting and decreeing to me, "There is *so much more* of Me to know, see, and experience." And then He spoke again, "Lana, you feel like you are going to explode—that's the point!"

Instantly, I was overwhelmed with His beautiful, incredible heart. What He sows and imparts into me, the encounters I have with Him, the moments of deep connection, all of those things rolled into one leaving me feeling like I am going to spontaneously combust—that's the point! He wants me to give away what I have! He wants me to release that which He has given me. He wants me in my sphere of influence to *overflow everywhere I go!* Part of that is leaning in to Him, remaining sensitive to the leading and prompting of His Spirit, and looking for Him everywhere I am going.

Learning to hear the voice of the Lord—and growing in sensitivity to His leading and His language—is an imperative part of our relationship with the Lord. It is for us to grow and know Him, but it is also for *the world*. It's for every person we encounter when we go out. That's really the nuts and bolts of what I want to look at in this chapter. But before we dive into that, I realized something profound in that powerful encounter I had with the Lord—what I *sow in overflows!*

STOKE YOUR FIRE

Stoke your fire! Sow in what you want to overflow. Build upon the areas you want to burn. What do I mean by this?

As you sow into your secret place, you will *release* what you *receive*. What you *take in* you will *let out*, so we all must continue to live our lives developing that beautiful continual conversation with the Lord that Brother Lawrence spoke about.

Your continual conversation with the Lord is a place you want to burn. It's a place I want to burn, and I need to be continually stoking my fire in that area, adding more and more fuel and wood to that fire to keep it burning. We want others drawn to the fire of the sweetness of His presence in our lives, drawn to His warmth and His fiery love. One of the most beautiful ways we can do that is to listen to what He is saying everywhere we go.

As a young believer, I would literally daydream about the day when the people of God were working with police—hearing from God and helping them solve crimes. I remember daydreaming about the people of God being positioned to minister to presidents to release the wisdom of heaven—God's people positioned like Daniel, like Esther, like Joseph. I would daydream of the days when God's people would walk into a coffee shop, hear God speak to them about someone in that place, and go and release the prophetic word, and the person would get saved, healed, delivered, set free.

As I got older, I went through Bible college. I read about revivalists of the past—stories like Charles Finney sitting on a train as it went through the station and people on the platform falling on their knees and repenting of their sins, coming to Jesus without anyone preaching to them. What I couldn't put words to back then I now can. The Lord was building a fire in me to see the supernatural realm of God, signs and wonders, and the power and love of God break *out* of the four walls of the church in my lifetime. The fire increased in me so much; everywhere I went I longed to partner with Him to see Him show up. I wanted the people of God (including myself) to hear Him in such a deep and intimate way that people's lives were being touched and changed as we went about our day.

Graham Cooke would tell stories about divine appointments he had in Starbucks or on airplanes when he heard from God and ministered to people—and I continued to burn!

I stoked my fire; I spent time with the Lord. I cried out for Him to teach me to hear from Him outside the four walls of the church. I read resources on hearing from God. I chose a few friends a week (without them knowing) and specifically asked the Lord for an encouragement for them, a prophetic word, and then I released it to them. I trained a lot in my own personal time with the Lord, stoking my fire, and then released that fire wherever I went.

I still remember the day when I realized that everything I was doing in my life to grow in hearing from God wasn't just for me—it was for others. I was sowing for someone else to receive. It changed my life! My heart burst with excitement, "Lord, who are You going to use me to speak to? What are You going to do through me?" I would dream *very* big. Then the rubber hit the road.

I was at Bible college and decided to get a part-time job, so I got a job in a Christian coffee shop. This shop was run by Christians who loved the Lord and had such a heart to see the Kingdom of God extended in the community and to impact the local area. I was elated! Not only did I get the amazing joy of making coffee for people all day long, but I was also working in a Christian environment.

I started working there, and things started to happen that took me by surprise. As I made coffee, sprinkling chocolate on the cappuccinos as worship music played all around me, I was connecting with Jesus over coffee. People would walk into the café, and I started feeling and hearing and seeing things for them.

A lady came in and I instantly had this strong feeling that God was going to release joy into her life. Another guy walked in close behind her, and I had a glimpse of a vision of the word *favor* written over his head. Another person came in and I felt such heaviness, sadness, and depression—God wanted to release peace over them.

All of a sudden, I was totally overwhelmed and afraid. I had burned and stoked my fire for *years* to move to a deeper level of partnering with Him in hearing His voice outside the four walls of the church, and now I was *freaking out*. Thoughts were running through my head: "Lord it was hard enough prophesying to people *in* the church. Now I am meant to tell someone *outside* the church something that You're saying? What if they're not a believer? What if they don't believe in prophecy? How am I going to say this so I don't sound like a weirdo?"

I wanted to run and hide in the cupboard with the coffee beans. Yet I felt the Lord so strongly and gently whispering to me and encouraging me that this is my next level of training. I just wasn't sure I wanted to be trained anymore. My heart was screaming, "What in the world was I praying for all those years!? Ahhh!"

The rubber hit the road!

It was one of those moments of decision. You know those places, those times? You have been crying out for so long for something, your heart burning and yearning for the *more*. Then you suddenly find yourself in that place—the open door, the divine breakthrough moment—and you're not sure you want to step in because you are *so* afraid.

Yep, that was me in a nutshell.

But I had a familiar feeling—that feeling I had when I first met Jesus and started hearing His voice. When God had me deliver a prophetic word to one of the other pastors in the church—that feeling visited me again.

So I had a decision to make. I felt like I was in the valley of decision. Again, the "what ifs" plagued me, so I slowly decided to put my toes in the water.

A Hiding Place Behind a Coffee Machine

For me, my toes in the water meant inching myself in *slowly*. I wanted to step out and be a voice outside the four walls of the church, and I wanted to stay in my comfort zone. Amidst the fear and crazy inner turmoil, I found my "hiding place" behind the coffee machine.

Thoughts would run through my head and heart: *"God, I want this so bad, I want to step out, I so long to see You move here in this place, but I'm petrified."*

But you know what? No matter how much fear I had, the fire and the hunger within me burned so much stronger than the fear. No matter how much fear screamed at me, "Don't step out and say anything, you might be wrong, you will look silly, what are you even going to say?" the fire of *what if God shows up* burned so much stronger.

So I started to pray into every cappuccino I made that God would show up and people would have an "out of the blue" encounter with God while they were sipping their coffee. That those who had never really even thought much about God would suddenly start to think about God as they drank their amazing cappuccino.

It might sound silly to you, but I really felt the Lord leading me slowly, with my toes in the water, by giving me a strategy to intercede and sow into others through my prayers without them even knowing. Crazy, amazing thoughts would flow through my heart and head. "What if I pray impartation of the love of God to be released every time I hand over a cappuccino to customers?"

Is God not big enough to do that? Of course He is big enough. I realized that where fear was trying to contain me and stop me from stepping out, the hunger inside me to release His voice everywhere I go was pushing me into His heart so much deeper to receive different strategies to minister outside of the church. I just didn't want to misrepresent the Lord. I didn't want someone to walk away and experience anything but the love, goodness, kindness, and hope of Jesus.

Certainly there are resources and tools that help us to hear the voice of God and release what He's saying and partner with what He is doing outside the four walls of the church, but I don't believe there is a specific "formula." I don't believe there is a one-size-fits-all formula to apply everywhere you go and God will show up.

BE SENSITIVE TO HIS STRATEGY

God knows individuals, and He knows the way they need to be ministered to and the way they need to receive Him. It's our responsibility to be sensitive to His strategy for the moment. So in that moment of beginning the next step of training for me in the coffee shop, the beginning strategy for me was intercession. So I was faithful to do that as much as I could.

It was amazing to see the little ways that the Lord honored those little steps. Handfuls of people started saying to me, "I want only you to make my coffee," and they'd have no idea why. Was I good at making coffee? I sure hope so! Do coffee lovers often have a favorite barista? Absolutely, I know I do, but I noticed the shift the moment I started to pray over those cappuccinos. I would daydream that as I made coffee the Holy Spirit was making glorious cappuccinos through me. After all, having come this far in this book, you would now know just how much the Lord loves meeting with me over a coffee. So why not anoint my coffee-making for His glory?

That's what I love about Him! He uses *everything!* Whether you pack shelves at a grocery store, make coffee for a living, are a mom at home and change so many diapers a day you lose count, or you're a lawyer, you're an accountant, you're a teacher—God has sent you into that place with the authority in His name to make a difference, to change the world one person at a time. I will say it again—*you are powerful wherever you go.*

So where were we? Coffee, of course! So I was praying into cappuccinos, releasing impartations, and seeing people all of a sudden drawn to me making their coffee and wanting to chat. For a while, the Lord trained me in interceding.

So many customers would get bathed in prayer over their morning cappuccino, and they never knew it. But you know what the Lord showed me so powerfully? *Every prayer, every word, every smile, every act of love, every act of kindness, every moment of engagement—whether with God or with a customer—was a seed that I was sowing into their salvation, their journey, their destiny, their life.*

Wow! The perspective of God! Wow!

THE "WHAT IFS" BEGAN TO SHIFT

The "what ifs" that plagued me in fear started to slowly shift in my perspective change. "What if the next prayer I pray, what if the next word of encouragement I release, what if the next smile I give, what if the next act of kindness I show sees the tipping point activated, the breakthrough moment of harvest when someone comes to know Jesus, gets healed, set free, delivered? What if?"

I began to think, "I want to live my life with the fearful 'what ifs' turned into the 'what ifs' of faith." One of Bill Johnson's powerful quotes that I absolutely love is, "You know that your mind is renewed when the impossible looks logical."

That was happening to me twelve or thirteen years ago, but I didn't have the language for it. My mind was being renewed; my heart and expectations were being expanded. "Could someone drink their cappuccino and have an encounter with Jesus and get saved without me even saying a word to them?" Some would say that's crazy talk! But I had the faith to see Him show up in a way that was out of the box.

"In a Christian coffee shop, where a well has been dug through prayer and intercession, could someone walk in with cancer and as soon as they hit the atmosphere of His presence, without anyone laying hands of them, they get radically healed?" My faith was exploding!

So the "what ifs" began to turn; my faith was increasing. I started to learn to "lean in" to the sensitivity and the feeling to pray that would come upon me when someone walked in. I would pay attention. Sometimes I felt fine and then, all of a sudden, someone walked into the coffee shop and I felt horribly depressed or fearful. At times I would be fine and happy, and the next minute a random thought of death would come into my mind. As I "leaned in" to Him and kept my fire well stoked with reading and listening to teaching on the prophetic, I realized that a lot of what I was feeling was not me. I was feeling the struggle of someone else or the atmosphere they carried. So I would begin to pray for them and decree the opposite, and often it would shift and lift.

If you are a seer and a feeler, you may enter rooms feeling fine, and once you walk in you start feeling weird things you didn't feel before. Someone might walk into your house and all of a sudden you start feeling depressed, highly anxious, or fearful. I want you to hear a few keys, especially with ministering outside the four walls of the church:

1. Pay attention to things that aren't your normal.

2. Don't run from it or take it on as your own.

3. Always ask the Holy Spirit what's going on. Always ask the Lord what He wants to do in that place, what He wants you to pray.

In my little coffee shop ministry world, sometimes I thought, "This caffeine is sending me up and down like a yoyo." Other times, I thought, "God is teaching me how to pray for others, follow His leading, and shift atmospheres."

I want to say, I am absolutely *no* expert on this subject. To this day there are times when I will be outside the church in my day-to-day life, and I pick up on atmospheres around me and have no idea what's happening. But the key is always the same key—*ask Him!*

That is why it is imperative and crucial that we know the Lord personally and we know how to hear His voice—so wherever we go we are leaning in for His strategy and direction. Dawna De Silva from Bethel Church in Redding, California has some *amazing* teaching on shifting atmospheres. I recommend if you find that's an area you really move in and experience, check out some of her teaching and stoke the fire of that gift God wants to grow in your life.

"STEP OUT OF THE BOAT, LANA"

I am so thankful that the Lord brings the right people into our lives at the right time for our journey.

That happened to me. I spent a substantial amount of time learning to "lean in" to the leading of the Spirit and voice of God outside of the church. The Lord was whispering, "Step out of the boat, Lana." The time had arrived. I am so thankful to God that as He called me to step out, He brought another employee to that coffee shop who had a lot more experience in the prophetic and the voice of God than I did. I shared my journey in parts as we started to get to know each other while frothing milk at the coffee machine, and then he started to push me out of my boat.

Every time we would work together, he would ask me, "What do you see over that customer?" I would be terrified. So I would share with him what I saw, and then he would say to me, "Well, go tell them!"

Now, I know that what God shows us is not all to be shared, but I *knew* that I *knew* that I *knew* that the Lord was speaking through this man. So I looked at a woman who had just paid for her coffee, and I heard three things:

1. "I love her."
2. "I have heard her cries and I haven't forgotten her."
3. "I am going to heal and restore her family."

She came over to take her coffee, and I didn't want to let go of the cup. It was the moment of decision. Do I share this word; do I not? I checked my word against First Corinthians 14:3:

> But when someone prophesies, he speaks to encourage people, to build them up, and to bring them comfort.

Okay—tick! Tick! Tick! The "what if" was creeping back in, but I was quickly reminded again of the "what if" of Him showing up and "what if" I say nothing and it's one of those tipping point moments.

So I let go of the cappuccino and released the word to her. It was very simple—I asked her permission first if I could share something encouraging with her. She said yes. I opened my mouth and said, "God really loves you. He has heard your cries, and He hasn't forgotten you, and He is going to heal and restore your family."

She looked at me quite blankly, and that few seconds without her response felt like a year. Then she began to cry. She wept as she looked at me and said, "This morning I asked God three questions. 'Do You love me? Are You hearing my cries? Have You forgotten me? Will You heal my family?'"

I couldn't believe it. I was over the moon! I was *so* excited! The Lord had showed up as I stepped out! Wow!

After I released that word, I was given other opportunities to minister to this lady one on one. It was such a beautiful moment.

From that point on I kept leaning in and learning and being continually intentional to ask the Lord what He was saying and doing in the coffee shop and everywhere I went. The key was to engage and then step out. I learned that releasing His words of life and encouragement to people didn't have to be weird.

I stayed away from the words "God said." I just purposed myself to be a person who spoke life, encouragement, and hope. I would hear His voice and release it as an encouragement. Many times, He would lead me to tell people that He loved them, so I would do that; other times, He would highlight something about the person to me, like "favor." I would simply say as I handed their coffee to them, "You know, there's some great days of promotion and favor coming to you." That would often lead them to asking questions or saying thank you.

I've heard so many stories of people releasing the prophetic word of God in an encouraging way, without "thus saith the Lord." Often, the question comes back, "How did you know that?"

TAKE THE PRESSURE OFF

I want to remove the pressure that might say you have to deliver a grand, huge prophetic word from God and have angels show up. That's amazing when it happens, but being a voice of hope and life and releasing the encouragement of God wherever you go is *so* powerful. Time and time again, when I don't know what to say I open my mouth and He fills it. So have fun with the Lord, seeking His heart and releasing words of life and hope.

I *always* gave glory to Jesus. I guess I had an advantage, working in a Christian coffee shop, because all the customers knew that we were Christians. I didn't try to hide the fact that Jesus was speaking; I was just sensitive to the Lord for *when* to say, "I really feel Jesus wanted me to tell you...." Some people who came in had been so hurt by the church that the name of God shut them down straight away. But the good coffee, huge play area, and friendly staff drew them in. So if I had started with the words, "I really feel Jesus wants me to tell you," the conversation would have ended. So I didn't operate by formula but by the Holy Spirit's strategy.

DON'T BE AFRAID TO ASK QUESTIONS

Sometimes God will show you a random picture, a vision, a verse, a feeling, and you have no idea what it means. If you press in and ask God for an interpretation but don't get anything, don't be afraid to *ask questions*. Engaging in a conversation with someone and asking questions to gauge whether you are hearing and discerning right can be helpful.

Many years ago, I was ministering to a lady and I felt so strongly the word *marriage* and then a strong sense God wanted to heal her marriage, but I had nothing else. I didn't know what to do. So I just blurted it out. Well guess what? She wasn't married! I could have saved a lot of awkwardness by asking her, "Hey, are you married?"

Asking questions and engaging in a conversation with the person can also be helpful in gaining greater discernment and insight of what God is saying as they share. Often, I have been given a word or a sense I don't understand, and as I have engaged in conversation with the person and asked questions, the Lord has given me more clarity. I know that the more you step out, the more God will give you.

In my coffee shop prophetic training ground, asking questions was a *very* helpful tool in growing in understanding what God was saying when He would show me something I didn't understand.

One thing I do always say is, when releasing prophetic words outside the church, avoid the words *God told me*. Those words lock people into a corner: "If God said it, then I can't argue with it." If the person doesn't agree with the word or doesn't feel it is right, it can leave them feeling that they are disobeying God and it doesn't give them the room to "chew it through."

ALWAYS SPEAK LIFE

I have often said throughout these chapters to always *speak life*. No matter what you see, feel, or hear, if it's negative, don't go and speak out the negative. Ask God for the answer. As Kris Vallotton says, "Ask for the redemptive answer."

I learned this very strongly and clearly one afternoon at the coffee shop. I had been ministering for a while, releasing words of life and hope. I was learning that if I saw something like depression or fear, I would speak the opposite—life, peace, hope, joy, breakthrough. I'd pray over them as they took their coffee—whatever He was leading me to do.

One particular day, I was making coffee, and my friend who had been pushing me out of the boat to prophesy more at work looked at me and said, "Do you see anything over anyone here today?"

I looked through the cafe and saw a young girl sitting having a coffee. I was instantly taken into a vision, and I saw a beautiful house; but all of a sudden I saw a huge shaking like an earthquake come and the foundations of this house started to break and the whole house started to crumble and came down to nothing. But where that house was built, another house started to be built, and it was twice as big and more beautiful than the one before. It was so beautiful. But do you know what I did?

I was so eager to not "miss" the opportunity to release a prophetic word and partner with what God was doing that I didn't ask Him, "What do You want me to do with what I see?" I just looked across to this friend of mine and told him what I saw. The word was delivered to the girl, and there was no amazing response, nothing—just a shaky, polite, "Uhh, okay thanks."

I was *so* excited that I had stepped out again. I went home that night, and I was full of joy that I had stepped out. Little did I know what was about to take place.

The next day was my day off, and my boss called me. He said to me, "Lana, did you give a prophetic word to a young girl yesterday about a house falling and being rebuilt?"

I replied so excitedly, "Yes, I did!"

My boss replied, "Lana, her mother called the coffee shop this morning and complained, because that word you gave her scared that young girl so much that she has been up all night crying and in fear."

In a moment my heart sunk. I couldn't believe it. What had happened? What did I do wrong? I was devastated that what was supposed to be a great encouragement was used to bring so much fear and pain upon someone. I wrestled, I cried, I talked to my boss and others, and then I realized what I had done wrong.

God showed me the house that was tumbling and crumbling down to nothing and the new house being rebuilt. The Lord didn't want me to share with this girl that everything she had ever known was about to be ripped out from under her. All she knew was about to come crumbling down to make room for the new thing God wanted to do in her life. As far as I knew, she wasn't even a believer. So not only had I portrayed a picture that her life was about to crumble, but also that there was a God in heaven who was about to do that to her and in her life.

I was crushed. Heartbroken. How could I have misrepresented Him in such a way? That situation, as hard as it was, as painful as it was, changed me because it taught me a *very* powerful lesson. Speak life, speak the answer, speak the opposite. Speak the redemptive answer of God. (Thank you, Kris Vallotton!)

The language around the delivery of that word should have been, "I see a completely new season upon you. There is a season where new things are being built in your life and they are going to be bigger than you have ever experienced. I see a real extension upon you, and there is going to be more blessing in your life than you have ever seen. Even if things change and don't look like they did, the new thing that is coming in your life is so much more beautiful and so much more amazing than anything you have walked in before."

That would have changed the whole situation. That would have brought hope, not fear. That would have breathed life and encouragement into her heart.

Our *delivery* of a word in the church and *outside* the church is *so* important, and that is a lesson that we all need to continue to learn and grow in. If we commit ourselves to always be ones who speak life, hope, and the answer, then we can't go wrong. Even in the "negative" stuff, press in and press through if you see it or feel it or sense it. Keep pressing in until you hear what the Lord wants you to do with it and how He wants you to steward it, whether by prayer or decreeing the answer to the problem.

Hear this—you are powerful wherever you go! His words of life, your prayers, your decrees are seeds released from the heart of God into the life of another. Remain teachable and sensitive to His Spirit. Everywhere you go, ask the Lord, "What are You doing here? How can I partner with You in this place?"

You are a world changer, and you are changing the world one person, one word of life, one random act of kindness, one encouragement, one prayer, one smile, one moment of sharing the Gospel at a time. You just never know what that one seed will do and the destiny of the person you are ministering to.

In the words of Heidi Baker, "Stop for the one." He stops for the one, and so should we!

See you in Chapter 10!

PRAYER

Lord, teach me to be sensitive to Your voice, Your leading, Your strategy everywhere I go. Lord, I pray for boldness and courage to step out and shine Your light wherever I go. Lord, I pray that You would give me greater insight, strategy, and sensitivity to be one who releases encouragement, life, blessing, and love everywhere I go. Jesus, teach me to love well. Teach me to love people in the church and outside the church as You would. Give me eyes to see others as You see them, to call out the gold within them. Teach me in greater ways to give away what You give to me. I pray, Lord God, that You would strengthen me to step beyond fear and walk in wisdom in releasing Your words of life, truth, and hope everywhere I go in Jesus's name. Amen.

DECREE

I am powerful everywhere I go because of whose I am. I am His. I decree that I have a voice and I have influence in every area in which the Lord has given me jurisdiction. I decree in the name of Jesus that I have the power to release life, hope, and encouragement everywhere I go. I decree that fear will not hold me back, but I will move as the Spirit prompts me. I will look for opportunities to call out the destiny and gold in others, to share the love of Jesus even through simple encouragement. I decree that I will not be silenced, but I can partner with Him in hearing His voice to speak His words and see His goodness and love extended everywhere I go, in Jesus's name.

CHAPTER 10

JEWELS OF ENCOURAGEMENT, IMPARTATION AND REVELATION

HELLO AGAIN!

What a joy it has been to journey with you through this book. What a joy it has been to partner with what God has wanted to give you, impart to you, release you from, awaken you to, and release you into as you have come on this journey with me of understanding the voice of God and encountering His heart.

This is our last chapter together! What a journey! I have cried, I have laughed, I have wrestled, I have decreed, I have prayed, I have worshiped, I have wept over the beauty of Jesus, I have jumped around in excitement, I have felt His touch deeper than ever, but most importantly I have fallen more in love with Him than ever.

I am going to invite you into my process with this book for a minute. I am going to bring you into a place of my heart and share with you what has touched my heart so deeply in my journey of writing this book. Do you know what it was?

It was the beautiful hand of the Lord and how He weaves and uses *all things*. *Nothing* is wasted, and He turns *all* things for good.

NOTHING IS WASTED

> *And we know that in all things God works for the good of those who love him, who have been called according to his purpose* (Romans 8:28 NIV).

> *So we are convinced that every detail of our lives is continually woven together to fit into God's perfect plan of bringing good into our lives, for we are his lovers who have been called to fulfill his designed purpose* (Romans 8:28).

I have lived this. In my life, I have lived these moments in so many ways. You know those times when you see how the Lord has worked everything for good and you get a glimpse of the beautiful masterpiece He has been creating? Well, friends, this book was that for me.

In writing this book, I have been overwhelmed with that revelation more than ever in my life. All of the little moments of saying *yes*, all of the moments I fell on my face and made mistakes, all the nights of being on my bedroom floor crying out, worshiping, so hungry to hear His voice, all the times when I was in such pain and frustration not knowing which way to turn or who could help me in my journey—but I continued to push through. All the times when I thought, "I am not going to make it," all the times the enemy came against me, all the times I sowed, I cried, I decreed, I prayed, every journey in hearing His voice even though they aren't all contained in this book, every step, every coffee with Jesus has led to, "For such a time as this!"

This book carries my heart. The words in these pages aren't empty words; I have lived them. These words I have written in these pages aren't just words, nice sentences, quotes, or things to "fill pages." The words on these pages represent so much of my journey with Him. They have been found, etched out, and received in some of the darkest nights, some of the most joyous mountaintop experiences, the most profound encounters, the hardest lessons and most painful processes, but He has used it *all*. I wouldn't have enough pages to tell you all the ways He has comforted me, shaped me, molded me, led me through, but this book has changed my life in a whole new way. This book has shown me at a deeper level than I have ever known that my Jesus, my beautiful Jesus, is the Master Weaver and that every process I have walked has not just been for me—it's been for others, it's been for you, it has been for the world.

Bill Johnson's words echo strongly in my heart more than they ever have before: "We owe the world an encounter with God." God is using my journey, my processes, my history with Him to build a beautiful demonstration of His glory, goodness, kindness, and love. I owe the world an encounter with God!

I felt the Lord wanted me to invite you into my journey in a deeper way through this book, but also release some key encouragements to you for your journey from this point on.

I want to encourage you that whatever journey you are on right now, whatever process you are walking through, whatever is going on, God is building something bigger than you can imagine. He is creating something more beautiful than you could ever know.

What He is planning is grander than you have even perceived. What you are walking through, the battle you are facing, my friend, it's not just for you. You are sowing daily through your relationship with Jesus into a testimony that is going to change someone's life. God is going to touch someone's life through your story, through your history with God. God's redemptive purpose will be demonstrated in your life in greater ways than you could ever imagine.

It is so important to continue to embrace the journey, embrace the process. Can I encourage you with that? You are not going to only have one moment in your life when you see the Master Weaver unveil His "behind the scenes" creation of your life; you will have many.

I feel His heart so strongly for you. I prophesy to you right now that whatever you are walking through, you are going to see Him as the Master Weaver in greater ways than you ever have. Stay in hope, stay in faith, because what He is creating behind the scenes is more beautiful than you know. Yes, even the messy part, the tears, the highs, the lows, the heart-wrenching battles and processes— all of it. He's making something beautiful out of the messes. Like a tapestry—if you look at it from the back where all the strings of cotton or wool are mixed together, they have knots in them and there's no beauty in it really, but when you turn it around it is *beautiful*.

Friend, you are going to have moments when the Lord is going to turn the tapestry around, and you are going to see the beautiful handiwork of God. *Everything, all things*, not just some things. Romans 8:28 doesn't say He works *some things* for good; it says He turns *all* things for good. *All things!* Whatever the enemy sends at you, what you walk through in life, the process of dying to self where you are taken deep into the fire of God—whatever it is, He will work it *all together* for good.

YOUR PROCESS IS POWERFUL

Please hear this today—*your process is powerful!*

What God is doing in your life right now, working together all things for your good, is preparing you in a greater way for the next steps that He has for you. So often, we try to rush process. So often, we are looking for the "exit stage left" in places of transition, because let's be honest—transition isn't comfortable at all. But it's in the place of process and transition that we see Him like we have not seen Him before. We are pushed closer to Him than we have ever been. We are brought to our knees in prayer as we cry out in our processes.

We are brought to our knees either in desperation and holding on to Him, or we are brought to our knees in *awe* of who He is and His goodness.

In the processes that we walk through in life, He works within us, He develops us, shapes us, and prepares us for the breakthrough and the promotion that comes after the process. In the amazing mountaintop seasons we are refreshed, strengthened, increased, built up, but the same goes for the valley seasons. In the valley seasons, we are strengthened, we are increased, we are built up, and we find our refreshment not from anything else but Jesus. In those deep, painful places, sometimes it gets to the point where we rely on Him for our every breath, for our next moment. We hold on to His Word so tightly to get us through the next hour. Whatever the process, He uses it all and He strengthens and prepares us.

Continue to embrace the process because He is working *for your good!* You may not understand what He's doing, you may not understand His way, but He is working out the plans for your life that are *good* (see Jer. 29:11).

GO DEEPER

I want to encourage you to go deeper than you have ever gone. I want to encourage you to sow into your relationship with Jesus like never before. Even as you read the words of this final chapter, I see the fire of God is going to fall upon you and release a greater impartation of hunger for Jesus upon you. I decree in the name of Jesus Christ that you are going to be hungrier for Jesus than you ever have been before.

The Lord has spoken to me so much over the last year about hunger and how the *hungry shall be fed,* so I decree over you in the name of Jesus that you are going to feast on the Word of God and the revelation He is releasing to you more than you ever have before. You are going to see the Holy Spirit take you into the depths of encounter with His heart like never before. I see the fire of God falling upon your eyes, upon your ears, upon your sensitivity to His Spirit right now, and you are going to encounter Him like never before. You are going to be plugged in more than ever to the leading of the Holy Spirit and the way that He is speaking in your life and through your life. I release right now an impartation for you to hear from God in ways that you never have before.

> His presence is not upon us to be commandeered or directed by us. Instead, we are tools in his hand. If there is a dove resting on my shoulder in the natural (and I love that phrase "and remained") and I don't want it to fly away, how am I going to walk around this room? Every

step will be with the dove in mind. Every movement I make will be to preserve what I value most.

—Bill Johnson, *Manifesto for a Normal Christian Life*

You know in Exodus 3 where Moses encounters the Lord as the burning bush? I have always loved that Moses *turned aside*. I have preached out of this story quite a few times over the past few years. He was commissioned from that place of radical encounter with the Lord and the burning bush. I *love* this verse:

> *When the Lord saw that he turned aside to see,*
> *God called to him out of the bush, "Moses, Moses!"*
> *And he said, "Here I am"* (Exodus 3:4 ESV).

Notice those first few words: "When the Lord saw that he turned aside to see." I believe that the Lord was waiting for Moses to turn aside. Today, I believe that the Lord is waiting for us to "turn aside" and to recognize something out of the ordinary—the obscure and unusual ways that He shows up. When we begin to see something different, we will stop and turn aside to see. God shows up in unexpected ways; He speaks in creative ways. I want to encourage you on your journey—continue to "turn aside." Continue to look for Him everywhere.

If you start to see Him move, speak, or show up in a way that is different from how you have encountered Him before, how you have heard Him before, don't keep walking, don't push it aside. Turn aside, lean in, press in, look for Him everywhere; you will hear Him call to you through the most incredible ways.

There is so much more upon you! There is so much more of His heart to seek out, there's so much more of His voice to hear, there is so much more of His Word to feast on. Like Bill Johnson says: "He is the Word of God, it is hard for Him to have nothing to say."

He is always, always speaking, and my heart fills with such joy as I write this because He has *so much more* that He wants to share with you. I prophesy over you that you are moving into a time when you are going to be left in *awe* of how He speaks to you and the *amount* that He speaks to you. I love what Heidi Baker says: "No matter how deep we have gone, there is *always* more."

There are depths of knowing Him and His heart before you that you have never experienced. That place of falling more in love with Jesus than you ever have. You just have to say yes. You just have to position yourself. Positioning is the key. Enjoy Him! Enjoy Him! Enjoy Him! Go have a coffee with Him, find your favorite place with Him, and lay down your life again, give Him your yes again. Give Him permission again to take you deeper than He ever has and speak to you in ways you have never experienced on His terms and His ways.

A whole new season of intimacy with Him will open up before you!

PURITY IN INTIMACY WITH HIM

I have such a passion for purity in intimacy. I have such a passion for seeing people so deeply in love with Him, living as laid-down lovers and really treasuring and stewarding His heart with integrity. At times I am brought to tears as in my own secret place with the Lord as I cry out, "Lord teach me to steward Your precious, beautiful heart with purity, integrity, and character." That very heart cry explodes from within me for others.

My heart burns with the prayer of David:

> *Lord, you can scrutinize me. Refine my heart and probe my every thought. Put me to the test and*

you'll find it's true. I will never lose sight of your love for me. Your faithfulness has steadied my steps (Psalm 26:2-3).

Examine me, God, from head to foot, order your battery of tests. Make sure I'm fit inside and out so I never lose sight of your love, but keep in step with you, never missing a beat (Psalm 26:2-3 MSG).

When I come before you, I'll come clean, approaching your altar with songs of thanksgiving, singing the songs of your mighty miracles. Lord, I love your home, this place of dazzling glory, bathed in the splendor and light of your presence! (Psalm 26:6-8)

Give the Lord permission to refine, probe our every thought, and put us to the test. We must be people who steward our own hearts and lives with integrity, purity, and character, and we steward our relationship and the heart of God with purity, integrity, and character.

I read a Bill Johnson quote once and it undid me because it was the fire that I carry articulated so beautifully in a few sentences.

God has called us into a place of tenderness, when nobody is looking, when there are no great decisions to make, when it's just him and me in a hotel room, with no one to pray for, no one to preach to. When it is just two people in a room, that's where you learn. That's where you learn his heartbeat. That's where you learn the presence. That's where you learn the voice. It's in the moments when nobody is watching, nobody is evaluating how good you're doing. When it is just you and him.

—Bill Johnson, *Manifesto for a Normal Christian Life*

Pursue His heart, not what He can do for you, not what He can give to you—pursue Him for who He is and commit yourself again to that beautiful place of tenderness before the Lord. When no one else is looking, can I encourage you? Invite Him! Allow the Holy Spirit to do whatever He has to do in your heart and soul to prepare you and shape you for all He has for you.

The Lord is continually looking for those who will steward His heart, what He speaks, and their lives with humility, purity, and integrity. He is looking for those who will seek Him above all else for no agenda other than to know Him and receive Him.

Part of the stewardship of His heart and our lives is to keep Him as our first love. To continually remain tender and sensitive to the workings of the Holy Spirit in our hearts, that we would allow Him to reroute our roots if they are found in anything else but Him.

Isn't this a beautiful quote by John Bevere: "Seek deeper friendship and intimacy with the Holy Spirit more than seeking His gifts."

I have been through many processes and lessons in my life regarding this very thing. The Lord has taken me through many *pits* to *prepare* me for the *position* that He had for me. He honored my prayer all the way through—that prayer that rose to heaven day after day: "Lord, I never want it to be about me; I want it always to be about You." I went through fire after fire where the Lord would show me areas of my heart where there was self-promotion, where there was agenda, where there was striving, and He would gently and lovingly reveal those areas to me and then take me into the fire. Did the fire hurt? Absolutely! Especially the one time many, many years ago when I thought I was going to be the next Joyce Meyer (and believe me, I didn't keep it to myself; I told everyone who would listen). I had the business cards printed; I had everything set up ready to take on the world and be the next Joyce Meyer, and what happened?

The Lord took me into a *pit*. You're probably thinking, "Hang on, did you just say *pit*, Lana?" Yes, I sure did.

He took me into a pit. He took me to a place where I had to ask a very real question. "Who am I without ministry? Who am I if I am not going to be Joyce Meyer? Where do I get my value if I never have a big ministry?" It was that moment when the seed falls to the ground and dies. Yep, that was a season of my life. But in that season, as painful as it was, He uprooted self-promotion, He uprooted striving, He uprooted it all.

I want you to hear this—He healed the *reason* that I was self-promoting, striving, and placing value in my ministry. He healed it. He showed me His love in such a deep and fresh way *in* that season and *from* that season on. That was one of the most painful seasons of my life; it lasted quite a long time, but you know what? Now I look back, and I am *so thankful* for that season. I am *so* thankful for what *He* did in my heart in that season. I needed to go through that process, that fire, to be able to carry what He has given me to carry now.

MATURITY COSTS SOMETHING

But the most precious thing was birthed in that season and has continued from that point is—I want His way or no way! I want to steward His heart, my relationship with Him, my life, my journey with purity, integrity, character, and humility. I want to embrace the fire of God in my life to choose Him and His way every time. I want to walk in maturity, not just gifting.

Gifts are free, but maturity is expensive.
—BILL JOHNSON, *Spiritual Java*

I want to walk in integrity, not just anointing. I want to walk in character, not just favor.

Joyce Meyer says in her book *A Leader in the Making*:

> You and I may have a gift that can take us places that our character cannot keep us. ...Gifts are given; character is developed. You must develop character so God can trust the way you will use your gifts.

My goodness—*so God can trust the way you will use your gifts!* We all want God to trust us and the way we use our gifts, the way we steward His heart, the way we steward our lives and relationship with Him.

I remember the times when I would be surprised by His voice, and He would so sweetly whisper, "I trust you." Those words changed my life, undid me, broke me, left me face down in worship of Him.

God is so amazing in all His ways. The thing is, it's not *my works* that built anything up in my own strength so He could trust me. It's His grace, it's His working in me, and His grace that enables me to partner with Him. My positioning to embrace the process and the fire. We must be good stewards, and we learn that in Matthew 25 and the parable of the talents.

CREATED TO LIVE IN CONTINUAL CONVERSATION WITH HIM

God's heart for you is to hear His voice and to live a supernatural life. To live in *continual conversation* with Him, living the calling He has placed over your life and operating in your giftings, flourishing in all He has for you. But He wants you to represent Him well. I love what Joyce said, that *character is developed*. No one can develop your character for you. That's between you and the Lord, but your character is developed in your process and the choices that you and I make, embracing His fire and process.

Friend, we must continue to sow into our intimacy with Jesus, but also continue to sow our *yes* into inviting Him to do whatever He needs to do, in whatever way He chooses, so that we are people who are the same out in public as we are behind closed doors. To live with integrity, we pay the price to allow the Lord to develop maturity in us and strengthen us. To live as people without agenda, but hearts that are laid down before Him and so in love with Him that we cry out, *"Lord, have Your way! It's for You!"*

Your gifting will take you a lot of places, but your character and intimacy with the Lord is your anchor that will you keep there. The Lord wants you to be able to carry what He is releasing—the giftings and plans He has for your life. He wants your maturity and my maturity to match our gifting. That requires time in the fire, but as you embrace the fire, as I embrace the fire, as we invite the Holy Spirit to teach us to live our lives with purity and integrity in stewarding His heart and His work within us, we will come out as pure gold carrying the greatest privilege of all—looking like Jesus!

THIS ISN'T THE END OF THE STORY

So here we are, nearing the end of this book, but this isn't the end of the story, your story. Your story with Him, your journey with Him will continue and you will walk many mountaintops. There will be valleys, but my prayer is that what you have received through my little puzzle piece of this manuscript in the divine, beautiful, huge puzzle of God has refreshed you, challenged you, and taken you deeper in Him. My heart is that you have fallen more in love with Jesus since you opened the first page of this book. My heart is so much that you saw Him, that you felt His love, that you heard His voice, that you found Him.

Because it is all about Him.

Again, I have so loved our journey. Thank you for coming on this journey with me. I want to ask something bold if I can.

Can we join together right now, not in "formulated" prayer, but in the prayer that bubbles up from the depths of our hearts, and give Him our *yes* again, together? Can we join together as siblings in the family of God and invite Him again? Invite Him into our journey from this point on. Whatever God has for us, wherever He leads us, the doors that He opens for us, the glorious things that He releases to us and through us—we will keep it all about Jesus.

REFRESH YOUR YES

Together, as children of God, we *refresh our yes!* Above all things, we invest into our secret place with Him. Remember the words that flowed from His heart that I shared with you in previous chapters: "Where are those who will linger?" Let us join together now and refresh our commitment to Him again to keep seeking His heart. To keep ourselves in that positioned place of intimacy.

The Lord is entrusting His secrets to those who will linger. He has so much more for you, so much more for me. Your history and my history with Him is a beautiful well.

I stand with you right now and I again *refresh my yes!*

I whisper the words of John Wimber: *"Come, Holy Spirit."* I whisper the words:

> *Come, Holy Spirit, in Your way, on Your terms, and do whatever You have to do in my life and through my life. May I know You more deeply than I have ever known You before. Come Lord, come Lord, I lay down any agenda, I make room for You, King of Glory, to come in like You have never come in before. I make room for You in my surrender, in my yieldedness. I invite You! I invite Your fire, Lord!*

> *Place this fierce, unrelenting fire over your entire being. Rivers of pain and persecution will never extinguish this flame. Endless floods will be unable to quench this raging fire that burns within you. Everything will be consumed. It will stop at nothing as you yield everything to this furious fire until it won't even seem to you like a sacrifice anymore* (Song of Songs 8:6-7).

As our journey together now comes to an end, I felt the Lord wanted me to end this book by sharing with you the words of a song. Yes, you heard right—the words of a song. It's a song called "A Whole New World" from the Disney movie *Aladdin*.

Let me say this straight up—I do *not* endorse magic, but do I believe that the Lord can speak through anything. Can He use a song from a kids' movie to speak to us—*absolutely!*

The Lord spoke to me profoundly through this song that it was a prophetic declaration of a whole new world of intimacy and encounter opening up before God's people. What I love in the movie is that before Jasmine gets on this magic carpet ride with Aladdin, he asks her a question: "Do you trust me?" She says yes, and she grabs his hand and goes on a magic carpet ride as the song plays.

I have released a prophetic word about "A Whole New World" for God's people encountering Him, hearing His voice, and breakthrough. I have read the lyrics to the song a lot while talking to the Lord about it. As I looked at the lyrics to this song, the Lord spoke many things to me, but the most profound of all was in that scene of the movie it wasn't about the *destination*. It wasn't about where that magic carpet was taking them.

It was about relationship; it was about the joy in the journey toward the destination. It was about going up higher and perspective shifting. Read the lyrics to this song as a prophetic declaration that a whole new world of intimacy in the journey is opening up for you. Your vision and sight is going to increase, and you will be more plugged in than ever to the strategy and perspective of His heart and the Kingdom of God. You will know greater joy in your relationship with the Lord than you *ever* have.

Friend, what a joy to dive into the depths with you!

> *The Lord bless you and keep you; the Lord make his face to shine upon you and be gracious to you; the Lord lift up his countenance upon you and give you peace* (Numbers 6:24-26 ESV).

Bless you, child of God!

Keep looking for Him everywhere!

A whole new world is upon you! Dive in!

PRAYER

*Lord, I refresh my **yes** to You again. Lord, I say **yes** to Your way, to whatever You want to do in my life. I trust You. Lord, I invite You to continue to do what You need to do in my life. I invite You, Lord, to shape my character; teach me continually about purity, integrity, and maturity. Lord, I embrace Your fire and Your Holy Spirit's work on my character and on my heart to examine my ways so that I may not only move in the giftings You have given me but the character and maturity to sustain it. Have Your way, Jesus, have Your way!*

DECREE

A whole new world of hearing His voice is opening up for me from today. A new level of awakening to His voice in my life and sensitivity to His Spirit. I decree that I will hear from God in new and fresh ways and there will be great **joy** and **adventure** in the new depths of hearing from Him. I decree in Jesus's name, "I am all in!"

ACTIVATION

I encourage you to go online and play the song "A Whole New World" and sit and journal with the Lord. Ask the Lord to give you vision and insight for the "whole new world" that He is opening up for you.

ABOUT
LANA VAWSER

Lana Vawser is first and foremost, a pursuer of God's heart and secondly, a prophetic voice to the nations. Her desire is to help people develop deep intimacy with Jesus and activate their prophetic hearing to recognize God speaking in everyday life. Lana is driven by a vision to see people set free and walking in the abundant life that Jesus purchased for them. She is an itinerant preacher and prophetic revivalist who gets to participate in powerful moves of God throughout the nations. Lana is married to Kevin and they live in Queensland, Australia, with their two sons.

OTHER BOOKS BY LANA VAWSER

Desperately Deep